My Tuscan Kitchen

My Tuscan Kitchen

Sunshine Manitto

NEW HOLLAND

Contents

Preface

I was so honoured when Sunshine asked me to write the preface for this book but how to capture the essence of the man, chef, teacher and friend?

I met Sunshine a few years ago in Italy on a cooking course where he was the chef. He inspired me with his passion for Tuscan cookery even though the most frequently heard phrase was 'più piccolo' (smaller) and oh the relief when I heard "basta!" (enough!). This patience and attention to detail is what makes Sunshine the chef he is. He cooks with his heart and it shows in the meals he produces. Simple ingredients become tasty, traditional plates of food; pleasing to the eye and to the mouth.

His passion and enthusiasm about using good, local produce is contagious. After going to Italy several times to learn more recipes I finally managed to persuade Sunshine to share his skills with some of my friends in Kempsey in England. He embraced this challenge and infected everyone who attended a lesson with his love for Tuscan cookery.

Grazie Sunshine per questo bel libro!

Liz

Introduction

This book was born from an idea, from the love and encouragement I receive from all the people who suggested I should start writing and creating cookery books. It's both a dream, and a game. It comes from my desire to communicate with the world through food.

It all started a few years ago during a cooking lesson when one of the participants looked me in the eye and said "You should write a cook book". I laughed, and didn't think twice about it for a while, not because I didn't think I was capable of doing it, but because I was so busy with my work. My art was cooking, creating both recipes and emotions. But over time, more and more people suggested I should write a book, until I eventually decided to take control of my communicative abilities and just do it. Thanks to all those people who ate food I prepared and got excited about it, I was inspired to open up to the world and communicate not just through my cooking courses or the food I put on the table, but through other channels, like this book, expanding my message and my vision beyond Italy.

During my cooking courses, the first thing I do is teach people to chop or dice ingredients very very finely, with a knife. Many people are surprised by this at first, or don't immediately understand why they need to learn this technique and why I make them do it, but they enjoy it anyway. I like to say "different chef, different obsession". Every cook has his or her habits and beliefs, techniques and style. It's like a personal fingerprint. One of my personal 'obsessions' is that of finely dicing the vegetables for frying at the start of a recipe, or the ingredients for filling fresh stuffed pasta, or meat that needs to be minced – I like to prepare food properly, with great care. When we eat, the sensations on the palate should be extremely pleasurable, an explosion of delicious taste and texture in the mouth.

So this has become the reassuring catchphrase, like a soundtrack that accompanies my cooking lessons – chop very finely, chop very finely… but when people taste the finished dishes they understand why I make them do this and they understand the importance of the care we must take when preparing food. It's fundamental, the ingredients need to be prepared as carefully as possible. Cooking is an art, but eating is also an art. The secret lies in the way these two arts are combined.

This book comes from the heart, with the deepest respect for Tuscany and its culinary traditions.

For the photographs, I chose to cook inside Tuscan houses and farms, using domestic kitchens instead of professional ones, in order to replace Tuscan cuisine in its proper context, to give it back its real soul and rustic identity. I make things, but I don't invent them. I personalise recipes, I change some ingredients but I respect tradition. Rarely do I turn a recipe upside down.

My art develops in the most magical locations in Tuscany, places where the history and beauty of this great land can be felt in all their glory.

This cook book contains simple recipes. I hope to have created a book that is full of energy and light. Practical, but also dynamic, a book that allows the reader to roam freely through it and inspires him or her to create. Together with my photographer I used every angle, every ray of light, every object and every Tuscan background imaginable to photograph my food. We decided there were no limits and we wanted to immortalise the dishes and our beautiful Tuscany – glorious land of food, poets and musicians, like Dante, Boccaccio, Petrarca and Puccini – in a book that bursts with beautiful images.

So, this is my first book and it is my introduction to good taste. Through the art of cooking, let your heart awaken, reinventing the peace and harmony that comes from feeling alive.

My cooking lessons and my philosophy in the kitchen

My cooking lessons are works of art, moments of profound meditation. It's hard to describe precisely how beautiful it is when people meet up at a cooking lesson. I aim to create a united group, because at the end of the day, we are all one thing together. There is no division between me and the group – we cook our lunches and dinners together in joy and harmony, glorifying taste and self-awareness around the dining table.

Everything starts with a complete Italian menu: starter, first course, main course, side dish, salad and dessert. The ingredients are of the best quality, organic if possible. Work stations are set out on the table: chopping boards-cuisine, knives, recipes and aprons, and then we begin our sacred dance.

We go round the table introducing ourselves, and it is very important that people know each other's names right from the start, as though they have been friends for ever.

Friendships are born immediately. We begin to prepare our ingredients, chopping them very finely, following our recipes. Then we go into the kitchen, where we cook our sauces and meats with vegetables and freshly prepared stocks.

We move on to preparing dessert, and then it is time to learn how to make fresh pasta, the most creative and spiritual part of the lesson. Accompanied by Italian opera music, the creative energy gently grows. The music is fundamental for me while we prepare the pasta. Nobody is left behind, we all help each other, and a perfect synergy is formed. There is no competition at my lessons, there is no competition in my kitchen, only synergy. Even though I am deeply grateful to the restaurant kitchens that were my training ground, I have already spent too many years in that kind of competitive and stressful environment. Now cooking is about joy for me. Life is always joy. In my Tuscan cuisine we use classic vegetable and fish stocks, some of them are my own inventions, and I avoid unnecessary use of animal fats.

Making fresh vegetable stock every day is important, and healthy. It's a wonderful and magical ritual. My cuisine is natural and follows the ever-changing rhythm of the seasons. It listens to the harmonious movements of the universe. Vegetable stock is the natural carburant that gives energy to my food and

is a balancing jump-starter for the digestive system. The first thing I do in the morning in the kitchen is prepare the vegetable stock.

Every lesson is different, even if I teach the same recipes. People bring wonderful energy, everything is grace and beauty. Someone once said that a teacher learns by teaching. My heart listens to other people's hearts, and so we give life to the process of creation of delicious food.

Joy and love are the secret ingredients for great results in the kitchen. I like to lose myself in this harmony with my students, giving birth not only to a cooking lesson but to a dialogue between people. It's a lesson in cooking, but also a lesson in life. I consider it a kind of miracle, this moment in which the most diverse group of people come together with one common goal, to learn to cook with feeling and awareness.

Importance is given to each ingredient and each person, giving the right value to the time we spend together. This is what we do at my lessons, learning to know each other and ourselves. I learn from my students, from their amazement and excitement, and all this makes me deeply happy. By teaching people how to cook I have grown both as a chef and as a human being. I am amazed by every lesson, as though it were always the first time I teach. Cooking is an intimate activity, and I am fascinated by doing it with people who I don't know. My profession is very demanding, but extremely enjoyable – it's like a theatre production, we each have a role that is important and contributes to the creation of our menu. The lesson is an all-round art, an evolution of emotions and preparation.

The kitchen buzzes with the sounds of people cooking, voices mingling harmoniously, moments of silence and concentration, laughter and energy, in an evolution of fragrance and sound. The environment is unique, and we have fun. Believe me, food cooked with joy is something else. We are what we eat, and our thoughts are important while we cook and then eat what we have prepared. When our thoughts are positive, life is decidedly better. I have radically changed my perspective, both in the kitchen and in my daily life. I have transformed my skills and begun a new journey, aware of and listening to the changes that life brings. This is fundamental for me, because we can change things for the better through our way of nourishing ourselves.

When we abandon our senses, we can live and cook with great energy and awareness. We are one with the universe, and if we can understand this we can cook beautifully, giving authenticity to each ingredient, personalising and enriching every dish we prepare. As an example, when different people prepare the same recipe, the ingredients may be exactly the same but the final taste of the dish changes from person to person. I'd like you to understand that it is essential to be genuine in the kitchen. Each one of us is special, and so is the food that each one of us cooks.

Starters

Cecina

INGREDIENTS

17½ oz/500 g chickpea flour

2½ pint/1.5 litres cold water

5 large pinches salt

10 tablespoons extra-virgin
   olive oil

Serves 6

Sift the chickpea flour into a bowl, add the salt and oil, then pour the water in gradually, whisking vigorously all the time to make sure there are no lumps of flour. The batter should be smooth and runny, neither too liquid nor too dense, but somewhere in between. Leave the batter to rest for at least 4 or 5 hours, or overnight if possible, stirring it occasionally. In summer it's best to keep it in the fridge. Preheat the oven to 220°C/425°F. Line a 12in/30cm circular baking pan with oven paper and grease it lightly with extra-virgin olive oil. Whisk the batter one last time and pour it into the pan to a height of about ¼in/½cm. Sprinkle with salt and black pepper, drizzle with oil and bake for about 10 minutes.

Our cecina is ready when it is golden, crispy on top and soft inside. Serve piping hot, with another optional sprinkling of black pepper.

This flatbread made of chickpea flour can be enriched with various ingredients, such as finely chopped zucchinis, asparagus, artichokes, green vegetables in general or cheeses such as pecorino, stracchino or gorgonzola.

It's simple and tasty, it's my favourite street food and I love it.

Panzanella

Superstition in the restaurant business in Lucca holds that servings in even numbers, particularly 2 and 4, are to be avoided. A bit like roses, which should always be presented in odd numbers. For this reason most of the recipes in this book are given in portion sizes to serve 5 people (depending obviously on how hungry they are!), but the quantities can easily be adjusted up or down.

INGREDIENTS

35 oz/1 kg bread
cold water
3¼ fl oz/100 ml white
   wine vinegar
7 oz/200 g red onion
   from Certaldo
3¼ fl oz/100 ml extra-virgin
   olive oil
17½ oz/500 g fresh ripe vine
   or San Marzano tomatoes
30 medium basil leaves
salt and black pepper to taste
optional medium sized cucumber

Serves 5

Cut the bread into 2in/5cm chunks, put them in a bowl and cover with a mixture of cold water and white wine vinegar. Squeeze the water out thoroughly and crumble the bread carefully. Once you have done this, slice the onion thinly, cut the tomatoes into 1¼in/3cm pieces, then mix the bread, onions and tomatoes together and season with olive oil, salt and pepper. Tear the basil leaves into pieces by hand (this is important) and add to the panzanella. The liquid from the tomatoes should also be added, then mix well and taste, and add more olive oil, salt and pepper if needed. Serve the panzanella in wooden bowls.

In the area around Florence and Pistoia cucumber is also added to panzanella. Other variations include tuna in olive oil or olives in brine, and a particularly good addition is cannellini beans cooked in a flask.

One note: the famous Certaldo onion is grown in this wonderful medieval village, which is also well-known for its annual Mercantia festival – a wonderful festival of street performers from all over the world.

Buttero Salad

A Buttero is a cowboy from the Maremma area of Tuscany. Thinking of their lifestyle and the simple local ingredients they could carry with them in their packs, such as bread, tomatoes and olives, I imagined this salad and christened it "Buttero".

INGREDIENTS

35 oz/1 kg bread
8 large ripe vine tomatoes
10½ oz/300 g Tuscan olives
   or Kalamata olives
30 basil leaves
10 tablespoons extra-virgin
   olive oil
5 pinches dried oregano
salt
black pepper

Serves 5

Cut the bread into ¾in/2cm cubes and spread them out in a baking pan. Sprinkle with olive oil and put in the oven at 200°C/400°F for about three minutes so the bread starts to toast. Take the pan out of the oven, stir the bread and then toast for another 3 minutes until it is a light golden brown.

While it's toasting, cut the tomatoes into wedges and mix them in a bowl with olives, oregano, basil leaves, salt and black pepper, then add the toasted bread cubes and mix everything together well. The croutons should be crunchy outside and soft inside. Add more olive oil to taste.

Serve this wonderful salad with a drink before dinner. Remember that the bread must be slightly warm when served in the salad to fully bring out the taste of this simple but delicious dish.

Marinated Sea Bass Carpaccio

INGREDIENTS

1 fresh sea bass fillet, about
   10½ oz/300 g
7 tablespoons extra-virgin olive
   oil
juice of ½ lemon
pomegranate seeds
salad lettuce
salt and white pepper

Serves 2

Cut the sea bass fillet into thin slices and put them in a bowl. Whisk the oil, lemon juice, 5 pinches of white pepper and 2 pinches of salt together to make a creamy emulsion. Pour the marinade over the fish and leave to rest for 3 hours. To serve, make a bed of salad lettuce, lay the slices of sea bass on top and pour the marinade over them. Garnish with pomegranate seeds.

This recipe is even easier than the previous one. Serve with fennel and carrot crudités.

Fennel, Orange and Almond Salad

INGREDIENTS

2 medium-sized fennel bulbs,
  about 7 oz/200 g each
2 ripe sweet oranges
½ lemon
¾ oz/20 g unpeeled flaked
  almonds
fennel fronds
½ oz/10 g toasted sesame
  seeds
5 tablespoons extra-virgin
  olive oil
salt and white pepper.

Serves 4

Wash the fennel, cut it in half then slice very thinly and arrange the slices on a large flat platter. Peel the oranges, remove the pith and chop the flesh into ½in/1cm cubes. Arrange the orange cubes on top of the fennel then sprinkle over the flaked almonds, fennel fronds and toasted sesame seeds.

Whisk the olive oil, lemon juice, a little bit of orange juice, salt and pepper until the mixture is creamy. Pour this dressing all over the salad. Serve the dish with an extra drizzle of olive oil and a sprinkling of black pepper around the edges of the dish. This salad is very refreshing for both palate and stomach.

Artichoke Carpaccio or "Segato"

INGREDIENTS

8 fresh artichokes, preferably
   purple
1 ½ lemons
5 oz/150 g parmesan or
   pecorino romano shavings
5 tablespoons extra-virgin olive
   oil
parsley
salt and white pepper

Serves 4

Clean and prepare the artichokes: remove all the tough outside leaves, cut off the thorns at the top of the artichoke hearts then cut them in half. Scrape out the hairs inside the hearts then slice them very thinly and put the slices in a bowl containing water and the juice of ½ a lemon.

Finely chop a couple of tablespoons of parsley. Drain the sliced artichokes and toss together with the parsley, olive oil, the juice of a lemon, salt and pepper, making sure the artichokes are well seasoned. Parmesan and pecorino romano are two very different cheeses, but both work well with the artichoke carpaccio so mix in shavings of the cheese of your choice. This is a very interesting salad that also combines well with smoked salmon. Try it!

Fried Stuffed Zucchini Flowers

INGREDIENTS

10 zucchini flowers (courgette)

3½ oz/100 g cow's milk ricotta

2 oz/50 g cow's milk
   mozzarella

1½ oz/40 g grated Parmesan
   cheese

¾ oz/20 g breadcrumbs

5 salted anchovy fillets

2 large eggs

3 pinches chopped parsley

flour

salt and pepper

1¾ pint/1 litre sunflower oil

Serves 5

Wash the zucchini flowers very carefully. Leave the pistil inside the flower, but remove the little green leaves around the base. Prepare the filling by mixing the parsley, ricotta, one egg yolk, finely chopped mozzarella, grated parmesan, breadcrumbs, salt and pepper. Beat the other egg with a pinch of salt. Fill the zucchini flowers with the mixture and half an anchovy fillet, then carefully close them by twisting the petals to seal. Dredge them in flour then dip into the beaten egg.

Heat the sunflower oil in a small pan about 8in/20cm in diameter. The oil should be deep enough to completely submerge the flowers. Fry them for 2–3 minutes, or until they are golden. Serve immediately while hot, with a green salad to refresh the palate.

Zucchini blossoms are beautiful flowers in the morning, a wonderful sight in the vegetable garden.

Farmer's Chicken Salad

INGREDIENTS

2 chicken breasts
   14 oz/400 g each
1 head red radicchio, about
   6in/15cm diameter
3 bunches rocket
3½ oz/100 g green
   radicchio or lettuce
3½ oz/100 g pine nuts
¾ oz/20 g celery
¾ oz/20 g carrot
¾ oz/20 g yellow onion
2 bay leaves
5 juniper berries
2 pieces of cinnamon stick
2 cloves
8 tablespoons extra-virgin olive
   oil
balsamic vinegar
salt and pepper

Serves 5

Cook the chicken breasts for about 40 minutes in lightly salted water with ¾ oz/20 g celery, ¾ oz/20 g onion and ¾ oz/20 g carrot, 2 bay leaves, 5 juniper berries, 2 pieces of cinnamon and 2 cloves. When the chicken breasts are cooked, drain and leave them to cool. Thoroughly wash the red radicchio, rocket and green radicchio (or lettuce) and chop finely. Cut the chicken breast into thin slices and chop coarsely. Mix the chicken and salad leaves together.

Zucchini, Basil and Nepitella Savoury Tart

INGREDIENTS

1 packet circular puff pastry,
   organic if possible

20 oz/600 g light green
   zucchinis (courgettes)

3½ oz/100 g yellow onion

3 sprigs of nepitella about
   6in/15cm long

7 tablespoons extra-virgin olive
   oil

20 basil leaves

vegetable stock no 4. (page 71)

4 nutmeg, white pepper, salt,

2 eggs

2½ oz/60 g grated Parmesan
   cheese

1 tablespoon white flour

Serves 5

Wash and dry the zucchinis, and dice into ¼in/½cm cubes. Chop the onion very finely and then fry it for about 3 minutes over a medium heat with 7 tablespoons of extra-virgin olive oil. Add the nepitella leaves and diced zucchinis, then add the basil leaves torn in half, salt, grated nutmeg and white pepper. Continue to cook for about 20 minutes, adding a little vegetable stock no.4. as needed. Take the pan off the heat.

Beat 2 eggs with a pinch of salt. Keep a little bit of this beaten egg aside and pour the rest into the pan with the zucchinis, adding the grated Parmesan cheese, and a tablespoon of flour. Mix well. Line a 10in/25cm circular baking pan or pie dish with oven paper and the puff pastry. Fill it with the zucchini mixture, then turn the edge of the pastry over the edge of the filling. Brush the pastry border with the beaten egg (or just use your fingers to smear it) so it develops a good glaze when cooked. Bake at 180°C/350°F for about 20 minutes.

This fresh and savoury tart is very popular at my public and private dinners, and is one of the best in its category. You won't have any leftovers.

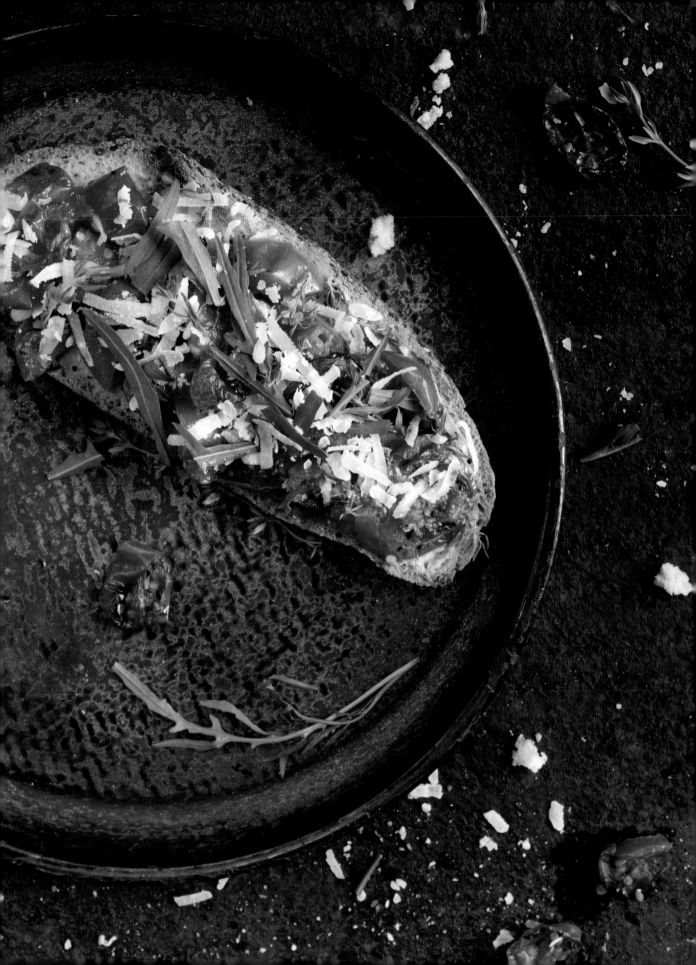

Crostini & Bruschette

Sausage and Stracchino Crostini

INGREDIENTS

10 slices bread, 2in/5cm wide
7 oz/200 g stracchino cheese
5 oz/150 g fresh pork sausage
extra-virgin olive oil
salt and white pepper

Serves 5

Smear the bread with olive oil and toast it in the oven at 200°C/400°F for about 4 minutes until it is golden brown. Squeeze the sausage meat from its casing and put it in a bowl with the stracchino cheese. Mash well with a fork, adding salt and white pepper to taste, until you have a smooth and well blended paste, and spread it on the warm toasted bread. There are two schools of thought with this particular recipe: one is to leave the sausage and cheese raw, while the other would be to put the topped toast back in the oven for about 4 minutes so the cheese melts and the sausage cooks slightly. I suggest you try both options. I like them both, so it's up to you to decide which you prefer.

Sweet and Sour Crostini

INGREDIENTS

10 slices bread, 2in/5cm wide

3½ oz/100 g pine nuts

7 oz/200 g raisins

1½ oz/40 g yellow and red
pepper (¾ oz/20 g &
¾ oz/20 g each)

2 tablespoons finely chopped
parsley

3½ oz/100 g bread soaked
in white wine vinegar

3 tablespoons extra-virgin olive
oil

salt and black pepper

Serves 5

Squeeze the vinegar out of the soaked bread and crumble it. Mix it with the pine nuts, raisins, yellow and red peppers and parsley, and chop everything very finely. Add the extra-virgin olive oil, salt and pepper, and mix well. Smear the bread slices with olive oil and toast in the oven at 200°C/400°F for about 4 minutes until golden brown. Spread the topping mixture on the warm toasted bread. As an optional addition you can drizzle a little acacia honey on the toast before adding the topping. This is a medieval style recipe.

Salt Cod Crostini Grosseto Style

INGREDIENTS

10 slices bread, 2in/5cm wide
10½ oz/300 g salt cod
celery, carrot and onion
3 cloves, 30 black peppercorns
¾ oz/20 g red pepper
¾ oz/20 g yellow pepper
2 tablespoons parsley
1½ oz/40 g salted capers
1 clove garlic
3 tablespoons extra-virgin
    olive oil
salt and white pepper

Serves 5

Stick 3 cloves into half an onion. Put it in a saucepan of water with a 4in/10cm piece of celery, a medium carrot and the peppercorns. Bring the water to the boil and boil the cod for about 10 minutes. Drain the fish and let it cool. Chop the garlic, parsley, capers and peppers very finely. Pick the flesh from the fish and chop it very finely as well, then mix everything together with 3 tablespoons of extra-virgin olive oil, salt and white pepper. Smear the bread slices with olive oil and toast in the oven at 200°C/400°F for about 4 minutes until golden brown. Top the toast with the fish mixture and serve warm.

This is an excellent starter for a seafood meal. Your guests will love it.

Tuscan Chicken Liver Crostini, My Style

INGREDIENTS

10 slices bread, 2in/5cm wide

10½ oz/300 g chicken livers

2 oz/50 g onion

1 medium clove garlic

1 bay leaf

1 sprig of rosemary,
 4in/10cm long

5 medium sage leaves

3¼ fl oz/100 ml dry white
 wine

Vegetable stock No. 2
 (page 70)

Serves 5

Finely chop the onion, garlic, sage and rosemary, and sauté with 5 tablespoons of extra-virgin olive oil for 5 minutes. Add the chicken livers, capers and bay leaf and cook until the liver changes shade. Add the dry white wine, and let it evaporate. Carry on cooking for about 30 minutes, adding vegetable stock no. 2 as necessary. The liver is ready when it can be broken into pieces by pressing lightly on it with a wooden spoon. Make sure the stock has evaporated or been absorbed, there shouldn't be much liquid in the pan with the liver. Remove the bay leaf, put everything in a blender and add the anchovy fillets, a knob of butter, 2 more tablespoons of extra-virgin olive oil, white pepper and nutmeg to your liking. Blend until the mixture is creamy, smooth and spreadable. Add a few drops of brandy or vin santo and blend again. Add salt if needed but be careful, the capers and anchovy fillets already provide a lot of salt, so don't go overboard with any extra. Smear the bread slices with olive oil and toast in the oven at 200°C/400°F for about 4 minutes until golden brown. These crostini can be served hot, which is better in winter, or cold in summer. Either way they are excellent as a starter to a meal, or a snack with an aperitif. Truly delicious, you won't be able to stop eating them.

Pecorino Cheese Crostini with Black Pepper and Truffle Oil

INGREDIENTS

10 slices bread, 2in/5cm wide
12½ oz/350 g pecorino
   cheese
30 black peppercorns
extra-virgin olive oil
a drizzle of white truffle oil

Serves 5

Smear the bread slices with olive oil and toast in the oven at 200°C/400°F for about 4 minutes until golden brown. Crush the black peppercorns with a pestle or meat mallet, and slice the cheese the same size as the toast. Cover each piece of toast with cheese and a sprinkling of black pepper. Put the crostini back in the oven at 200°C/400°F for about 4 minutes.

Serve your toast with a drizzle of white truffle oil and sigh with delight.

I usually use an oil from San Miniato near Pisa, which produces a highly prized truffle. The aroma and taste will take your breath away.

Classic Fresh Tomato Bruschetta

INGREDIENTS

5 slices bread, 6in/15cm wide

5 fresh, ripe vine tomatoes

1 large clove garlic

20 medium basil leaves

5 tablespoons extra-virgin
  olive oil

dried oregano

salt and black pepper

Serves 5

Smear the bread slices with olive oil and toast in the oven at 200°C/400°F for about 4 minutes until golden brown. Cut the tomatoes into ¼in/½cm thick slices. Rub each slice of warm toast with the unpeeled garlic clove and arrange the sliced tomatoes on top. Sprinkle with salt, pepper, a pinch of dried oregano and a drizzle of olive oil. The basil leaves can be used whole as a garnish for the bruschetta, or torn coarsely and scattered on top. Serve your bruschetta immediately – it is a simple and classic dish that everyone enjoys. To vary the presentation, try cutting the tomatoes into half-moon shapes or diced into cubes.

This is the more modern bruschetta that has evolved over time from the authentic and ancient Tuscan recipe, which consisted simply of toasted bread rubbed with garlic and rubbed with ripe tomatoes, dressed with salt, black pepper and oil. In fact ripe tomatoes are known in Tuscan jargon as 'rubbing tomatoes'. The original version is very 'poor', but it gave rise to subsequent variations, so why not try it?

Tuscan Kale Bruschetta

INGREDIENTS

5 slices wholemeal bread,
  6in/15cm wide
17½ oz/500 g Tuscan kale
  or black cabbage (braschetta)
3 cloves garlic
5 tablespoons extra-virgin
  olive oil
salt and black pepper

Serves 5

Wash the kale and cut it into small ¾in/2cm pieces. Blanch it in lightly salted hot water for about 5 minutes and drain, conserving the water as it will be needed for the recipe. Sauté 2 whole cloves of garlic in extra-virgin olive oil, then add the kale and fry for at least 5 minutes with some ground black pepper and salt. If it sticks to the pan add a little of the cooking water as necessary. Smear the bread slices with olive oil and toast in the oven at 200°C/400°F for about 4 minutes until golden brown. Rub the unpeeled garlic clove on top of the toast, top with the kale and serve hot or warm. For a non-vegetarian version, put a slice of lard on top of the garlic bread, put it back in the oven at the same temperature of 200°C/400°F for about 1 minute and then top with the kale.

This is a very simple bruschetta, but unforgettable and authentic in both versions.

Black cabbage or braschetta is a widely used ingredient in Tuscan cuisine, very popular in the countryside and frequently used in soups. From the nutritional point of view, it has a high vitamin C content.

Stracchino, Asparagus and Carrot Bruschetta

INGREDIENTS

5 slices bread, 6in/15cm wide

7 oz/200 g of stracchino or
crescenza soft cheese

2 medium carrots

5 asparagus spears

4 tablespoons extra-virgin
olive oil

salt and black pepper

Serves 5

Cut the carrots into ¾in/2cm long matchsticks and do the same with the asparagus including the tips. Sauté the vegetables in a pan with extra-virgin olive oil for about 4 minutes over a medium heat, add salt and pepper to taste. Then mix the vegetables and cheese in a bowl with salt and black pepper. Smear the bread slices with olive oil and toast in the oven at 200°C/400°F for about 4 minutes until golden brown. Rub the toast a little with the garlic clove, then spread the cheese and vegetable mixture on top. Put the bruschetta back in the oven at 200°C/400°F for about 2 minutes.

Serve hot – these simple and tasty bruschetta are delicious.

Bruschetta With Gorgonzola, Walnuts and Chestnut Honey

INGREDIENTS

5 slices bread, 6in/15cm wide

14 oz/400 g soft gorgonzola
  cheese

1 clove garlic

10 medium-sized walnuts

chestnut honey (mountain
  flower honey)

Serves 5

Smear the bread slices with olive oil and toast in the oven at 200°C/400°F for about 4 minutes until golden brown. Rub the warm toast with the unpeeled garlic clove, then spread the gorgonzola on the toast, and open the walnuts and put 2 or 3 pieces of kernel on top of each slice. Put them back in the oven at 200°C/400°F for just 2 minutes. Remove from the oven and serve your bruschetta topped with a drizzle of chestnut honey.

I love this bruschetta! It is a great winter recipe.

In recent years in Tuscany, chestnut honey has been rediscovered and is now back on our tables. To me, chestnut trees are like majestic and wise statues.

Grain Salads

Spelt Salad With Vegetables and Senese Pecorino Cheese

INGREDIENTS

9 oz/250 g pearled spelt

3 oz/80 g carrot

1½ oz/40 g celery

2½ oz/60 g Tropea red onion

3 oz/80 g light green
   zucchinis (courgettes)

3½ oz/100 g semi-mature
   pecorino cheese

6 tablespoons extra-virgin
   olive oil

2 tablespoons white wine
   vinegar

2 tablespoons balsamic vinegar

20 medium basil leaves

salt and white pepper

Serves 5

Rinse the spelt and cook it in boiling salted water for about 30 to 40 minutes (depending on type of spelt), then rinse and cool it with cold water. Finely dice the celery, carrot, onion, zucchinis and cheese into tiny cubes the same size as the spelt grains. Mix everything together and season with olive oil, white wine vinegar, balsamic vinegar, salt and white pepper. Tear the basil leaves into 3 pieces, add to the salad and mix again. Serve your salad as a starter or first course.

Instead of spelt, you could also try this recipe with brown rice, cracked wheat or barley.

Of course, when using grains they should be whole grains and organic in origin. This very simple salad has a strong and refreshing taste.

Spelt Salad With Red Radicchio, Tuscan Olives, Frisée and Lemon Zest

INGREDIENTS

9 oz/250 g pearled spelt

1 head red radicchio
  about 5 oz/150 g

3½ oz/100 g frisée salad
  leaves

7 oz/200 g olives

1½ oz/40 g lemon zest

2 oz/50 g zucchini (courgette)

25 cherry tomatoes

6 tablespoons extra-virgin
  olive oil

4 tablespoons balsamic vinegar

salt and black pepper

Serves 5

Rinse the spelt and cook it in boiling salted water for about 30 to 40 minutes (depending on type of spelt), then rinse and cool it with cold water. Julienne-cut the red radicchio and the frisée leaves. Cut the tomatoes into quarters, grate the lemon zest and chop the olives. Dice the zucchini into tiny cubes the same size as the spelt grains.

Mix all the ingredients with the cooled spelt, and dress the salad with salt and black pepper, balsamic vinegar and extra-virgin olive oil. Mix again and serve garnished with a whole leaf of radicchio and curls of lemon peel.

Summer Salad

INGREDIENTS

9 oz/250 g pearled spelt

14 oz/400 g fresh cherry
  tomatoes

30 medium basil leaves

9 oz/250 g fresh pecorino
  cheese

3 teaspoons dried oregano

5 tablespoons extra-virgin
  olive oil

parmesan cheese shavings to
  garnish

salt and black pepper

Serves 5

Rinse the spelt and cook it in boiling salted water for about 30 to 40 minutes (depending on type of spelt), then rinse and cool it with cold water. Cut the tomatoes into quarters, the cheese into small cubes, and gently tear the basil leaves in half. Mix everything together with the cooled spelt and dress the salad with extra-virgin olive oil, oregano, salt and black pepper. Garnish with parmesan cheese shavings.

This is an easy to prepare salad for outdoor dining and picnics in the summer. I like to make it this way, which is the Tuscan version using pecorino cheese, but it can also be done with ordinary cow's milk mozzarella and if you wish you can add some black olives. Classic taste, very Italian, genuine and always stylish.

Spelt Salad With Artichokes, Vegetable Ragù, Black Olives, Rocket and Asparagus

INGREDIENTS

9 oz/250 g pearled spelt

4 purple artichokes

8 medium-sized asparagus
spears

20 olives in brine

3½ oz/100 g rocket leaves

5 oz/150 g of vegetables for
ragù (celery,carrot, onion,
zucchini (courgette))

6 tablespoons extra-virgin
olive oil

½ lemon

2 tablespoons red wine vinegar

salt and white pepper

Serves 5

Rinse the spelt and cook it in boiling salted water for about 30 to 40 minutes (depending on type of spelt), then rinse and cool it with cold water. Clean the artichokes down to the hearts (remove the external hard leaves, all the thorns and the hairs inside), slice them thinly and put them in cold water with the juice of the half lemon. Slice the asparagus into discs, cut the olives into quarters and finely chop the vegetables (celery, carrot, onion, zucchini) into a diced ragù. Drain the artichokes, mix everything with the cooled spelt, then dress the salad with extra-virgin olive oil, red wine vinegar, salt, white pepper and mix in the rocket leaves. This salad is a carnival parade of bright and intense ingredients, one after the other, and it's perfect for the spring with all those raw and crunchy vegetables. I'll give you one little variation for a seafood twist – add 5 oz/150 g of shrimps, blanched in boiling water and lemon juice.

Spelt Salad With Shrimps and Sea Asparagus

INGREDIENTS

9 oz/250 g pearled spelt

25 oz/700 g peeled
  king shrimps (prawns)

5 oz/150 g sea asparagus
  (samphire) or wild asparagus

1 lemon,

15 fresh cherry tomatoes

3 tablespoons chopped parsley

3½ oz/100 g carrot

3 oz/80 g celery heart

3½ oz/100 g zucchinis
  (courgettes)

6 tablespoons extra-virgin
  olive oil

salt and white pepper

Serves 5

Rinse the spelt and cook it in boiling salted water for about 30 to 40 minutes (depending on type of spelt), then rinse and cool it with cold water. Put the king shrimps in a pot of lightly salted boiling water with half the lemon for about 3 minutes. Drain and leave to cool. Blanch the asparagus in boiling salted water. Cut the carrots, celery heart and zucchinis into julienne sticks and cut the cherry tomatoes into quarters. Mix the cooled spelt with all the other ingredients, dress the salad with 6 tablespoons of extra-virgin olive oil and the juice of the remaining half lemon, and season with salt and pepper. You can decide if you need to add more lemon or salt or white pepper, to your own taste. This salad is very nutritious with many health-benefitting properties, and the recipe is well balanced. With its elegant and sublime taste, it is perfect for special occasions.

Legume Salads

Chickpea and Salt Cod Salad

INGREDIENTS

10½ oz/300 g dried chickpeas

14 oz/400 g salt cod

2 tablespoons chopped parsley

6 cloves garlic

6 sprigs rosemary

1 small dried chilli pepper

4 tablespoons white wine vinegar

6 tablespoons extra-virgin olive oil

salt and white pepper

Serves 5

Soak your chickpeas for 12 hours in cold water with a pinch of salt, then cook them in boiling salted water with 5 cloves of unpeeled garlic and 5 sprigs of rosemary about 4in/10cm long. The chickpeas, when cooked, should be soft but whole and not falling apart. When they are ready, drain and cool them under running water. Very finely chop a clove of garlic, the chilli pepper (cayenne), and a sprig of rosemary. Mix with the chopped parsley and then stir everything together with the chickpeas. Cook the cod in unsalted water because the fish is already very salty. Boil the cod for about 10 minutes, then drain and leave it to cool down slowly. Don't rinse it with water or you will rinse away the sublime taste of the sea! When the fish is cool, remove the flesh and mix it with the chickpea salad. Dress with extra-virgin olive oil, white wine vinegar, salt and white pepper and mix again. This delicious salad should be served cold and it works well in all seasons. The herbs and spices are intense, and I guarantee that your guests will be highly impressed when you serve it as a starter or side dish in a seafood menu.

Cannellini Bean and Citrus Salad

INGREDIENTS

10½ oz/300 g dried
 cannellini beans

6 cloves garlic

20 sage leaves

10½ oz/300 g cherry tomatoes

5 tablespoons lemon peel

5 tablespoons lemon juice

2 tablespoons white wine
 vinegar

3 tablespoons chopped parsley

6 tablespoons extra-virgin
 olive oil

salt and black pepper

Serves 5

Soak your cannellini beans for 12 hours in cold water, then cook them in lightly salted boiling water with 6 cloves of garlic and 20 sage leaves. The beans, when cooked, should be soft but whole and not falling apart. When they are ready, drain and cool them in cold water. Cut the tomatoes into quarters, chop the parsley very finely and cut the lemon peel into very thin strips. Mix everything with the beans and dress the salad with extra-virgin olive oil, white wine vinegar, lemon juice, salt and black pepper. Mix again gently and serve in small earthenware bowls. I like to play and experiment with the appearance of the food I prepare – having fun with the presentation inserts life and energy, and it is like painting a picture. This is a refreshing dish, with its citrus tones.

Borlotti Bean and Certaldo Onion Salad

INGREDIENTS

10½ oz/300 g dried
  borlotti beans
6 cloves garlic
20 sage leaves
3 oz/80 g Certaldo red onion
4 tablespoons finely chopped
  parsley
4 tablespoons white wine
  vinegar
6 tablespoons extra-virgin
  olive oil
salt and white pepper

Serves 5

Soak your borlotti beans for 12 hours in cold water, then cook them in lightly salted boiling water with 6 cloves of garlic and 20 sage leaves. The beans, when cooked, should be soft but whole and not falling apart. When they are ready, drain and cool them in cold water. Chop the onion and parsley very finely and add them to the beans, then dress with extra-virgin olive oil, vinegar, salt and white pepper and mix gently with your hands.

Every type of salad, whether it's leaf, legume or cereal based, should be mixed with the hands – just as people always did in the past, when we weren't scared of touching food.

Serve this bean salad with small slices of toasted bread. It's a quick and easy recipe, but it has great character and intense taste.

Green Bean and Shrimp Salad, Lucca Style

INGREDIENTS

20 oz/600 g small shelled
    green beans

14 oz/400 g fresh shrimps
    (prawns)

7 oz/200 g cherry or
    Piccadilly tomatoes

4 tablespoons chopped parsley

1 lemon

6 tablespoons extra-virgin
    olive oil

1 small dried chilli pepper

salt and white pepper

Serves 5

Buy canned green beans, organic if possible. If you can't find them then use dried beans, soak and cook them. Every now and then it's acceptable to use quality tinned products, don't you think? Blanch the shrimps for 3 minutes in very hot water with a little salt and half a lemon. Drain them and leave to cool. Cut the tomatoes into 8 parts and chop the parsley and chilli pepper, very finely as always. Put the green beans, tomatoes, shrimps, chopped parsley, chilli pepper and the juice of the remaining half lemon into a bowl, season with salt and white pepper and gently mix everything with your hands.

I will say no more about this recipe – just try it, and include it in a seafood menu, where it will be well loved and appreciated.

Vegetable and Seafood Stocks, and Aromatic Oils

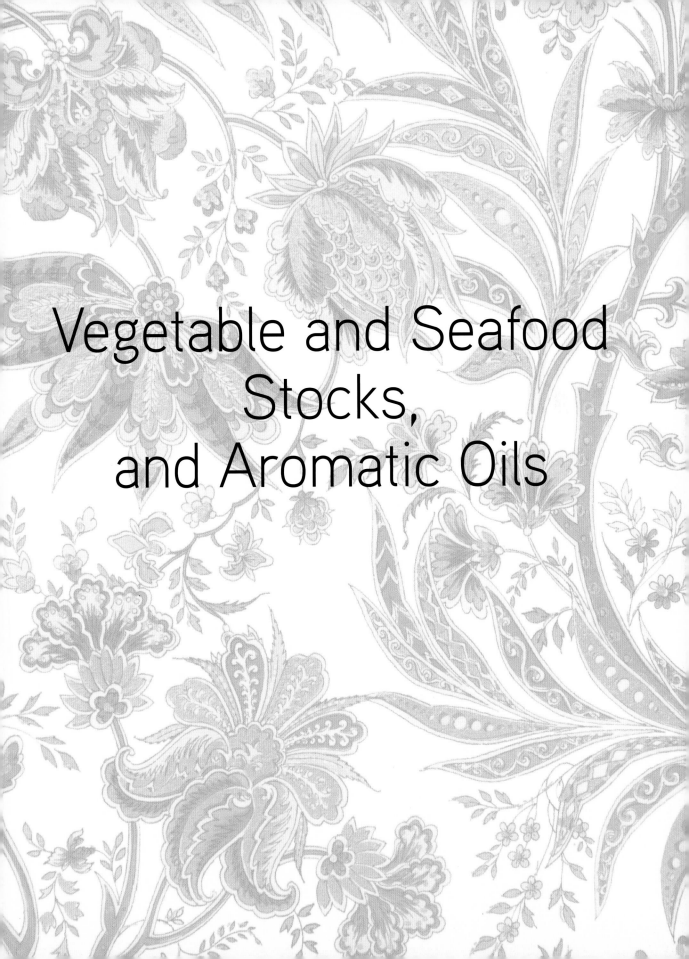

1 Basic Vegetable Stock

For every 6¼ pints/3 litres of cold water use a stick of celery, a whole carrot and a whole onion. The weight of each ingredient is about 3½ oz/100 g. Add a small handful of salt. Bring the water to the boil with the vegetables and salt, and after it has boiled for 20 minutes it is ready to use.

This stock is the simplest of all and can be used for everything, from lengthening soups to braising meat and fish, quick-cooking recipes such as escalopes, fish fillets, etc. It's a generic base stock.

If you make it at the start of the week, it will keep in the fridge for 3 to 5 days. Obviously it would be better to make it fresh every day, but those who don't have time for this can do it every 5 days at the most. When it has completely cooled to room temperature, put it in an air-tight container and keep it in the fridge. My personal opinion, and my philosophy in the kitchen, is to cook with vegetable stock, or at the most fish stock. Even when preparing a meat or poultry dish I prefer to use vegetable stock, because it creates a natural balance within the recipe. When we eat a poultry dish like chicken cacciatora, the vegetable stock aids the digestion process. On the other hand, when we eat a meat dish prepared with meat stock or chemical stock cubes, digestion takes longer and is more complicated. Test my opinion – it costs nothing. We need to return to natural foods and avoid those that are industrially produced. This is obvious.

2 Vegetable Stock With Onion, Cloves and Parsley

Stick 5 cloves into an onion that weighs about 3½ oz/100 g. Put it in a pot with 3½ oz/100 g celery, 3½ oz/100 g carrot, a small bunch of parsley and some salt. Pour in 8½ pints/4 litres of water and bring to the boil. I usually use this vegetable stock for lengthening soups or for rich stewed meat and aromatic fish dishes. The cloves have an intense, strong taste and this stock adds a delicious taste to any recipe. You can use it for mixed-grain soups, chickpea soup, Tuscan braised wild boar, meat ragù, duck ragù or pigeon risotto. It should be used in recipes that contain cloves, cinnamon, juniper berries or other particular spices. As we journey through this book we can experiment, test, and decide. I have suggested this stock for specific recipes but this does not prevent you from trying it in others.

My cuisine is all about synergy – I believe in the beauty and the balance of ingredients. Have no fear in the kitchen. Dare to experiment, while respecting certain rules.

3 Enriched Vegetable Stock

Put 3 oz/80 g celery, 3 oz/80 g carrot, an 3 oz/80 g onion, 2 medium potatoes around 3½ oz/100 g and 2 vine tomatoes (cut in half or quarters), a small bunch of parsley and some salt into a pot. Pour in 8½ pints/4 litres of water and bring to the boil. Due to the addition of potato, tomato and parsley we can use this stock for vegetable soups such as ribollita, frantoiana, pappa al pomodoro, spelt soup, fresh tomato sauces etc. For poultry dishes we can use it in chicken cacciatora, guinea-fowl with porcini mushrooms etc. It's good for all recipes that contain potatoes and tomatoes, fresh or tinned.

4 Garden Vegetable Stock

This is the previous enriched vegetable stock with the addition of 3 oz/80 g zucchinis (courgettes), 2 oz/50 g fennel bulb and 2 sprigs of fennel fronds. It's halfway between the enriched stock and a simple minestrone soup, and is good for all vegetable soups and stews, vegetable sauces, stewed meat with vegetables and braised fish with vegetables. It can be used in any recipe really, but is particularly suitable for dishes with a predominance of white and green vegetables. The fresh tomato in this stock is relatively little and it doesn't override the other ingredients. It can also be blended and eaten as a cream of vegetable soup, adding a drizzle of extra-virgin olive oil and some freshly ground black pepper.

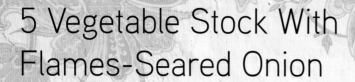

5 Vegetable Stock With Flames-Seared Onion

This stock is the same as the basic vegetable stock (no.1), with the difference that the onion is cut in half and lightly seared over a flame. When the onion is prepared in this way it gives a particular taste and aroma to the stock, which we can use for all game meats, porcini mushroom risotto, mixed meat stews and sauces for pork products such as sausages. Use it for braising fish such as salt cod, herring and mackerel. The onion should be just seared and certainly not burned, to avoid it giving a bitter taste to the stock.

6 Fish Stock and Concentrated Fish Stock

There are an infinite number of recipes and variations for fish stock, but I will give you the simplest one that still packs a punch. Put 3 oz/80 g carrot, 3 oz/80 g onion, 3 oz/80 g celery, ½ oz/10 g parsley and two unpeeled garlic cloves into a saucepan. Add 20 oz/600 g of fish scraps, such as scorpion fish, gurnard, sea bream or sea bass, including the fish heads. Don't use tuna or swordfish. Add salt and a handful of black peppercorns, pour in 6¼ pints/3 litres of cold water and bring to the boil. Simmer for about one hour and then filter through a fine mesh strainer. This stock can be used for all fish dishes.

The ingredients for a concentrated fish stock are basically the same, with the addition of a glass of dry white wine with the water. Simmer the stock for about two hours and filter it, then put it back on the heat for another 30 minutes. You can also add an optional half lemon with the other ingredients. The concentrated stock is suitable for all fish dishes, including risottos, seafood pasta sauces and braised fish.

I would say that the first recipe is a fish and vegetable stock, which is then transformed in 'fumetto di pesce' or seasoned and concentrated stock by the extended cooking process of the second recipe. Have fun experimenting with both versions in your fish dishes.

7 Shellfish Stock

Roughly chop 3 oz/80 g celery, 3 oz/80 g onion, 3 oz/80 g carrot and ¾ oz/20 g parsley. Heat 3 tablespoons extra-virgin olive oil in a frying pan, and add the vegetables with 17½ oz/500 g of shellfish scraps – heads and shells of shrimp, scampi or crab. Fry gently for 10 minutes then add 3¼ fl oz/100 ml of brandy. When the brandy has evaporated, add 8½ pints/4 litres of water, a piece of lemon rind, sea salt and a small handful of peppercorns. Bring to the boil, simmer for about one hour and then filter. Use this 'fumetto di crostacei' or seasoned and concentrated stock for all shellfish recipes. The taste is intense and sweetly aromatic.

Aromatic Olive Oil For Grilled Meats

INGREDIENTS

20 tablespoons of extra-virgin
  olive oil

8 sage leaves

3 sprigs rosemary

2 cloves garlic

10 sprigs fresh thyme

10 sprigs marjoram

½ lemon

salt and black pepper

*Recipe for 35 oz/1 kg of grilled
red meat or pork or lamb*

Finely chop the sage, rosemary, garlic, thyme and marjoram. Put the chopped herbs in a bowl with the extra-virgin olive oil and squeeze the lemon over everything. Add salt and black pepper, and this is the perfect aromatic olive oil for grilled meats – steak or beef tagliata with herbs, grilled pork or lamb chops. It is simple, but simply exquisite!

Aromatic Olive Oil For Roast Meats and Vegetables

Finely chop 2 medium garlic cloves, ½ oz/10 g fresh thyme and ½ oz/10 g fresh marjoram. Use a pestle and mortar if you have one, otherwise chop very finely with a knife. Mix together with ½ oz/10 g good quality dried oregano, salt and black pepper to taste, or as we say in Italian Q.B. – "quanto basta". Mix everything with 10 tablespoons of extra-virgin olive oil.

Use this oil to season 70 oz/2 kg of potatoes and then roast them in the oven at 200°C/400°F for 30 minutes to get potatoes that are crunchy on the outside and deliciously soft on the inside. You can also use this aromatic oil for seasoning mixed roast vegetables, which then go in the oven at 200°C/400°F for about 25 minutes.

Use the same recipe but double the ingredients for 70 oz/2 kg roast ham or lamb, to serve 8 people. Smear the meat well with the aromatic oil, then put it in a roasting pan with 2½ oz/60 g celery, 2½ oz/60 g carrot and 3 oz/80 g onion chopped into ¼in/½cm pieces, and moisten everything with 10 fl oz/300 ml of dry white wine. Put it in the oven at 170°C/325°F for about 2 hours, and as the meat roasts, turn it and baste it every now and then with a little vegetable stock. When it is cooked, purèe or blend the vegetables with the meat juices from the pan. Cut the meat into ¼in/½cm slices and serve with the gravy made from the vegetables and aromatic oil. Words cannot describe how delicious this roast is – you have to try it!

Aromatic Olive Oil For Salads and Meat Or Fish Carpaccio

There are so many ways to dress fresh salads and meat or fish carpaccio, but I really like a traditional method with a little variation.

Example: take 10 tablespoons of Tuscan extra-virgin olive oil, 2 pinches of salt, ground black pepper and the juice of half a large lemon. Beat vigorously together using 2 forks or a whisk until it becomes a fairly creamy emulsion. This fresh dressing can be used for salads and beef carpaccio, or for a raw vegetable oil dip. If you put the same ingredients in an electric blender you will get a very dense and creamy sauce which is ideal for smoked fish carpaccio such as salmon, swordfish and tuna, and also for fresh fish carpaccio, such as sea bream, sea bass, cod and fresh lean salmon.

Slice your fillet of sea bream, sea bass, cod or salmon very thinly. Cover the slices with this creamy dressing and leave to marinate for 3 to 4 hours, after which the flesh will be very tender. Always use the freshest fish possible. Substitute white pepper for the black pepper and the taste will be more delicate. You can also try a trio of black, white and pink pepper. With a few small variations, this recipe is ready to use.

Chopping very,
very finely

In this chapter I will use two Italian words that have no single-word equivalent in English. They are simple concepts, but absolutely essential if you want to reproduce genuine Italian recipes successfully:

Battuto – a very finely chopped mixture of fragrant raw vegetables and/or herbs and other ingredients, which provides the delicious base for a recipe. From the Italian verb 'battere', meaning to strike or beat.

Soffritto – the word for the same finely chopped raw mixture when it is sautéed in olive oil or butter or any other fat. From the Italian verb 'soffriggere', meaning to fry gently.

I would like to say a few introductory words about this chapter, which will give you foundations and ideas for creating your own recipes. In Italian cuisine, and cooking in general, we have the opportunity to create, to use our imaginations. I don't mean a situation of total anarchy, but a conscious anarchy in the kitchen.

In pastry-making we cannot be flexible with weights and measures – haute patisserie has to go on the scales, as we say here in Tuscany. In other forms of cooking, on the other hand, we have rules but we also have a margin of freedom to vary our dishes and recipes. I love this, because it allows you to cook creatively, where the basic recipe has to be respected but every recipe can be personalised or customised without ruining it.

The wonderful thing is that cooking, in this case Tuscan cuisine, teaches us to love it and make it our own. What I really want to convey to you is that when we cook we can admit to our mistakes, and we can carry on cooking without feeling guilty, and it is quite likely that new recipes will be born from our mistakes. To explain myself better – I teach Tuscan cuisine and the secret is to love ourselves and love food and life.

I wanted to write these few lines to make it clear to myself and to all the people who read this book that the most important secret in the kitchen is to respect what you do and love what you do. We are human and we make mistakes – and that's quite something for me to say, because I am a person who finds it hard to admit his own mistakes. I'm very strict with myself, but this book is an opportunity for me to change. Change is wonderful. This chapter is very important, mainly because this is the chapter that gives you the foundations for creating new recipes yourselves. To me, this is a beautiful thing, and I hope it will be the same for you.

BASIC Battuto NO.1

The basic battuto in Italian cuisine, in this case Tuscan cuisine, is composed of celery, carrot and onion.

These are the three basic ingredients of this base, and I call them prince celery, queen onion and princess carrot. This battuto enables you to make tomato sauces for any kind of pasta, braised meat and fish dishes. Let me give you some examples:

EXAMPLE 1

INGREDIENTS

2½ oz/60 g celery,

3 oz/80 g onion,

3 oz/80 g carrot

8 tablespoons extra-virgin olive oil

17½ oz/500 g organic tinned chopped tomatoes

25 basil leaves

a pinch of brown sugar to balance the acidity of the tomato

salt and white pepper

Chop the celery, carrot and onion very finely. Fry in extra-virgin olive oil for 5 minutes, then add the tomatoes, basil leaves, pinch of sugar, salt and white pepper. You have a fresh tomato sauce for pasta. If you put meatballs or fish into this sauce, it's a different dish, and if you add some chilli pepper to the diced vegetable base, it's a different dish yet again.

EXAMPLE 2-With meat

INGREDIENTS

2½ oz/60 g celery

3 oz/80 g onion

3 oz/80 g carrot

8 tablespoons extra-virgin
olive oil

35 oz/1 kg beef cut into
1¼in/3cm cubes

2 tablespoons plain flour

7 fl oz/200 ml red wine

3½ oz/100 g organic tinned
chopped tomatoes

vegetable stock no.1 (page 70)

black pepper

nutmeg

salt

Serves 5

Chop the celery, carrot and onion very finely and fry in 8 tablespoons of extra-virgin olive oil for 5 minutes. Flour the meat and brown it in the pan for 8 minutes. Pour over the red wine, let it evaporate a little and then cover the meat with vegetable stock no.1. Add the tomatoes, black pepper, nutmeg and salt, and cook for about 1 ½ hours. You can use lamb, goat, veal, duck or pork.

EXAMPLE 3-With fish

INGREDIENTS

2½ oz/60 g celery

3 oz/80 g onion

3 oz/80 g carrot

8 tablespoons extra-virgin olive
oil

17½ oz/500 g organic
tinned chopped tomatoes

3 small dried chilli peppers

3 pieces of salt cod, about
9 oz/250 g each

2 tablespoons chopped parsley

a little salt

Serves 3

Chop the celery, carrot and onion very finely and fry in 8 tablespoons of extra-virgin olive oil for about 5 minutes. Add the tomatoes, cook for 15 minutes and then add the salt cod. Cook for another 15 minutes. You could use cuttlefish or squid instead of salt cod, and add some potatoes. Once again, starting from the same basic recipe you will obtain a completely different result, a new recipe. These are just a few ideas but you can also experiment with other ingredients.

Battuto NO.2

Celery, onion, carrot, capers and pine nuts.
This battuto can be used with vegetables and fish, plain or with tomatoes. It can also be used with meat in more spicy recipes. Let's have a look at some examples which will help you to experiment and create something new.

Example 1
Mixed pan-fried vegetables

INGREDIENTS
2 oz/50 g celery
3 oz/80 g onion
3 oz/80 g carrot
20 salted capers
1½ oz/40 g pine nuts
6 tablespoons extra-virgin
   olive oil
7 oz/200 g yellow pepper

7 oz/200 g zucchini (courgette)
7 oz/200 g eggplant
   (aubergine)
5 oz/150 g fresh cherry
   tomatoes
20 basil leaves, white pepper,
   salt

Serves 5

Wash your vegetables and cut them into 1¼in/3cm cubes. Chop the celery, onion, carrot, capers and pine nuts very finely, and fry for about 5 minutes in 6 tablespoons of extra-virgin olive oil.

Then add the cubed vegetables (yellow pepper, zucchini, eggplant) and cook for about 10 minutes on a high heat. Add the cherry tomatoes, basil leaves, salt and pepper and cook for another 10 minutes. This is just one example – you can vary the vegetables and other ingredients. Use oregano or marjoram instead of basil and the result is a different dish. Then try adding potatoes, cauliflower, artichokes…

Example 2-With fish

INGREDIENTS

2 oz/50 g celery,

2½ oz/60 g onion

2½ oz/60 g carrot

30 capers

1½ oz/40 g pine nuts

2 tablespoons chopped parsley

1 dried chilli pepper

6 tablespoons extra-virgin
    olive oil

3 pieces of salt cod, about
    9 oz/250 g each, or very
    fresh salmon or tuna or
    swordfish

5 fl oz/150 ml dry white wine

vegetable stock no.5 (page 72)

white pepper

a little salt

Serves 3

Chop the celery, onion, carrot, capers and pine nuts very finely, mix with the finely chopped parsley and fry everything for about 5 minutes in 6 tablespoons of extra-virgin olive oil. Lightly flour the salt cod pieces and add to the pan, when they have browned a little pour over the white wine and evaporate it. Add salt and pepper to taste (go easy with the salt, as the cod is already very salty) and cook for about 15 minutes, adding a little vegetable stock as necessary.

Example 3-With meat

INGREDIENTS

3 oz/80 g celery,

3 oz/80 g onion

3 oz/80 g carrot

30 salted capers

1½ oz/40 g pine nuts

42 oz/1.2 kg stewing meat
    cut into ¾in/2cm cubes
    (beef or veal or pork)

6 tablespoons extra-virgin
    olive oil

7 fl oz/200ml prosecco
    (sparkling dry white wine)

10½ oz/300 g organic
    tinned chopped tomatoes

3½ oz/100 g black olives in
    brine

vegetable stock no.2 (page 70)

2 tablespoons turmeric
    (or 2 teaspoons saffron), salt

Serves 5

Chop the celery, onion, carrot, capers and pine nuts very finely, then fry in 6 tablespoons of extra-virgin olive oil over a medium heat for about 5 minutes. Add the cubed meat and brown it, then pour over the prosecco and evaporate it a little. Cover the meat with vegetable stock no.2, then add the olives and tomatoes and cook for about 30 minutes. Add the 2 tablespoons of turmeric (or 2 teaspoons of saffron), salt to taste and cook for another 45 minutes. When the meat is buttery-soft and tender, it is ready. Another example for you to experiment with.

Battuto NO.3

Celery, onion, carrot, capers, pine nuts, garlic
This battuto is very similar to the previous one, but with the addition of garlic,
and it's suitable for similar recipes such as pan-fried vegetables, braised meat and
fish dishes. You could also substitute almonds for the pine nuts.

Example 1

INGREDIENTS

2½ oz/60 g celery
3 oz/80 g onion
3 oz/80 g carrot
2 medium garlic cloves
20 salted capers
1½ oz/40 g pine nuts

7 tablespoons extra-virgin
 olive oil
42 oz/1.2 kg eggplant
 (aubergine)
5 oz/150 g organic tinned
 chopped tomatoes
white pepper, salt

Serves 5

Wash your eggplants and cut them into 1¼in/3cm cubes. Put them in a bowl with 3 generous pinches of salt, which will cause the eggplant to release the bitter liquid it contains. Meanwhile, chop the celery, onion, carrot, garlic, capers and pine nuts very finely and fry everything in 7 tablespoons of extra-virgin olive oil for about 5 minutes. Drain the eggplants from the liquid they have produced and add them to the pan. Cook for another 15 minutes and then add the tomatoes, white pepper and salt. After another 10 minutes and you can add herbs such as basil, oregano, marjoram or thyme, as you wish. Wonderful fragrance and wonderful taste! Try using zucchinis or a mixture of fresh vegetables.

Example 2

INGREDIENTS

2½ oz/60 g celery

3 oz/80 g onion

3 oz/80 g carrot

2 medium garlic cloves

20 salted capers,

1½ oz/40 g pine nuts

7 tablespoons extra-virgin
olive oil

35 oz/1 kg squid or cuttlefish

5 fl oz/150 ml dry white wine

20 oz/600 g floury potatoes

2 tablespoons chopped parsley

vegetable stock no.3 (page 71)

2 dried chilli peppers, salt

Serves 5

Wash and clean the squid or cuttlefish and cut into 1¼in/3cm pieces. Chop the celery, onion, carrot, garlic, capers, pine nuts and chilli peppers very finely, and fry everything with 7 tablespoons of extra-virgin olive oil for about 5 minutes. Add the squid or cuttlefish, and cook for another 5 minutes, then pour over the white wine, evaporate it, and continue cooking for at least 40 minutes, adding vegetable stock no.3 as necessary. Cut the potatoes into 1¼in/3cm pieces and add to the pan. Cover and simmer over a medium-low heat until the potatoes are cooked, again adding vegetable stock as necessary. When you can easily pierce a potato with a fork, it's done. Stir in the chopped parsley and serve. Delicious!

Battuto NO.4

This battuto is made with celery, onion, carrot, sage and rosemary. Ideal for those who are garlic-intolerant, but if that's not the case then feel free to add 1 medium garlic clove. This battuto is important for braised dishes, such as the various ragù made with beef, lamb, duck or pigeon, and also for cooking game meats. It's suitable for meat, but not for fish, because the sage and rosemary are too strong. But that's just my opinion - always remember, different chef, different opinion. This is the beauty of diversity.

Back to our battuto, following the usual procedure.

Example 1

INGREDIENTS

2½ oz/60 g celery

3 oz/80 g onion

3 oz/80 g carrot

1 sprig rosemary 6in/15cm long

4 sage leaves and 1 fresh
  bay leaf

8 tablespoons extra-virgin olive oil

35 oz/1 kg lean lamb cut into
small ½in/1cm cubes

5 oz/150 g organic tinned
chopped tomatoes

7 fl oz/200ml dry white wine

vegetable stock no.2 (page 70)

black pepper, nutmeg, salt

Serves 5

Chop the celery, onion, carrot, sage and rosemary very finely, and fry in 8 tablespoons of extra-virgin olive oil for about 5 minutes, then add the lamb cubes. Brown the meat, pour over the dry white wine and evaporate a little. Cover the meat with vegetable stock no.2, add the bay leaf, tomatoes, salt, black pepper and nutmeg. Cook for about an hour with the help of more vegetable stock as needed. The meat is ready when it is soft and the sauce is creamy. You can use it to dress fresh egg pasta such as maccheroni, tagliatelle or pappardelle, or make a saffron risotto, with asparagus if you like, and serve it together with the lamb as a single dish.

Example 2

INGREDIENTS

3 oz/80 g celery

3 oz/80 g onion

3 oz/80 g carrot

1 sprig rosemary

4 medium-large fresh sage leaves

7 tablespoons extra-virgin olive oil

42 oz/1.2 kg venison or other
  game meat

10 fl oz/300 ml red wine,
  vegetable stock no.2 (page 70)

20 juniper berries, 2 bay leaves

black pepper, salt

Serves 5

Chop the celery, onion, carrot, rosemary and sage very finely, and fry in 7 tablespoons of extra-virgin olive oil for about 5 minutes, then add the juniper berries and sage leaves. When the vegetables have softened, add the venison cut into 1¼in/3cm pieces and brown it for 10 minutes. Pour over the red wine and evaporate it a little. Add salt and pepper to taste then continue cooking with the help of vegetable stock no.2 for about 1 hour and 30 minutes. When the meat is soft serve it piping hot with ottofile polenta or slices of toasted bread. A different recipe again, built on the foundations of the same battuto. Remember, this works for any kind of braised game meat.

Battuto NO.5

Onion, garlic, capers, pine nuts, red pepper.
This fifth and final battuto can be used for vegetables, pasta dishes and some meat recipes, but above all for fast-cooking fish recipes. Let me give you some examples. This book contains a recipe for a vegetable side dish, my Val d'Arno peperonata. You can use the same method for potatoes or for a mixed vegetable dish. Here's a more detailed example.

Example 1

INGREDIENTS

3 oz/80 g onion

2 medium cloves garlic

15 salted capers

1½ oz/40 g pine nuts

2 oz/50 g red pepper

7 tablespoons extra-virgin olive oil

35 oz/1 kg mussels or clams

5 fl oz/150 ml dry white wine

2 tablespoons chopped parsley

salt and white pepper

14 oz/400 g spaghetti or fresh
   egg
tagliatelle pasta

Serves 4

Chop the onion, garlic, capers, pine nuts and red pepper very finely, and fry in 7 tablespoons of extra-virgin olive oil for about 2 minutes. Then add the shellfish, cover and cook for 3 minutes over a high heat. Add the wine and after another 8 minutes add the chopped parsley, a pinch of salt and white pepper. Take off the heat. Cook the pasta in boiling salted water, and drain it 2 minutes before the end of cooking time, reserving a little of the cooking water. Put the pasta in the pan with the shellfish, and finish cooking it with the help of a little of the pasta cooking water as needed. Toss well to make sure it's thoroughly mixed and serve your creation piping hot. You can use other types of shellfish or fish, such as mullet, salt cod, salmon, gurnard etc.

Example 2

INGREDIENTS

3 oz/80 g onion

2 medium cloves garlic

15 salted capers,

1½ oz/40 g pine nuts

2 oz/50 g yellow pepper (you
can swap between yellow, red
and green, as you wish)

1 tablespoon chopped parsley

7 tablespoons extra-virgin olive oil

3 fish fillets such as sea bream,
sea bass etc, about
7 oz/200 g each

5 fl oz/150 ml dry white wine

7 oz/200 g fresh cherry tomatoes

15 fresh basil leaves

Serves 3

Cut the tomatoes into quarters. Chop the onion, garlic, capers, pine nuts and pepper very finely, and fry for about 2 minutes in 7 tablespoons of extra-virgin olive oil. Flour the fish fillets, add them to the pan and fry for about another 3 minutes. Pour over the white wine and cook over a high heat for 8 minutes. Add the tomato quarters, basil leaves, chopped parsley, white pepper and salt. Cook for about another 3 minutes and the fish is ready when the sauce is creamy. Serve with a side dish of green beans or mixed green salad or roast potatoes.

Example 3

INGREDIENTS

2½ oz/60 g onion

2 large cloves garlic

20 salted capers

1½ oz/40 g pine nuts

1 oz/30 g yellow pepper

1 oz/30 g red pepper

6 tablespoons extra-virgin
olive oil

35 oz/1 kg white meat (lean
pork or chicken)

2 tablespoons finely chopped
parsley

5 fl oz/150 ml prosecco

vegetable stock no.3 (page 71)

black pepper, salt

Serves 4

Chop the onion, garlic, capers, pine nuts and peppers very finely, and fry in 6 tablespoons of extra-virgin olive oil for about 2 minutes. Cut the meat into 1¼in/3cm pieces, add it to the pan and brown it. Pour over the white wine, evaporate a little, and continue to cook using vegetable stock no.3 as necessary. Add salt and white pepper to taste. If you use pork, the cooking time will be longer, about 1½ hours, whereas chicken will be ready in 40 minutes. This is another example of how you can use this battuto.

We have looked at many possibilities and variations in this chapter. I want to make it clear that we must always experiment and try things out in the kitchen. Create, within reason. Have fun, and enjoy what you do.

Soups

Tuscan Mixed Grain Soup, Lucca Style

INGREDIENTS

17½ oz/500 g mixed dried
  grains and legumes (peeled
  broad beans, shelled peas,
  red and green lentils, black-
  eyed beans, barley, spelt,
  azuki beans)

3 oz/80 g celery

3 oz/80 g onion

3 oz/80 g celery

2 large cloves garlic

1 sprig rosemary
  6in/15cm long

10 medium sage leaves

1 clove

1 small piece cinnamon stick

3½ oz/100 g organic tinned
  tomatoes

6 tablespoons extra-virgin olive
  oil

salt, white pepper and nutmeg

Serves 5

Chop the celery, carrot, onion, garlic, sage and rosemary very finely, then fry gently in a steel or terracotta pot with 6 tablespoons extra-virgin oil over a medium-low heat for 10 minutes. Rinse the grain and legume mix in cold water and add it to the pot. Stir well for about a minute to mix all the ingredients, then add 2½ pints/2 litres of warm water. Add the tomatoes, squeezed out by hand and chopped. The soup will be liquid but after one hour of cooking, it will be denser. Add salt, white pepper and nutmeg to taste. Add vegetable stock if the soup becomes too thick. If it does start to stick to the pot, take it off the heat immediately and let it cool down for a while. The grains attached to the pot will unstick when you put it back on the heat. The soup is ready when the black-eyed beans and broad beans are soft. It's up to you whether you prefer a liquid or dense soup, but either way it should have a creamy consistency. Serve it with croutons sautéed in a pan with a drizzle of extra-virgin olive oil or toasted in the oven at 200°C/400°F for 5 minutes. Those who eat meat can add 2 oz/50 g of lard or smoked bacon to the chopped vegetables at the start of the recipe. This soup is excellent in all seasons.

I am very attached to this recipe – it was my first, and is perhaps the only one that has been with me for more than 20 years.

Chickpea soup

INGREDIENTS

10½ oz/300 g dried organic
   chickpeas

3 sprigs rosemary and 3 large
   garlic cloves for cooking the
   chickpeas

2½ oz/60 g onion

2½ oz/60 g carrot

2 oz/50 g celery

2 large cloves garlic

10 medium sage leaves

2 sprigs rosemary
   6in/15cm long

1 clove

1 small piece cinnamon stick

2 oz/50 g organic tinned
   chopped tomatoes

6 tablespoons extra-virgin olive
   oil

vegetable stock

salt, white pepper and nutmeg

Serves 5

Soak the chickpeas for at least 12 hours or overnight in cold water with a tablespoon of bicarbonate of soda or salt. The next day, cook the chickpeas in 6¾ pints/3 litres of salted water with 3 sprigs of rosemary and 3 unpeeled garlic cloves. Cook them until that they are soft but not falling apart. Meanwhile, chop the celery, onion, carrot, garlic, sage and rosemary very finely, and fry in extra-virgin olive oil with the whole clove and piece of cinnamon for about 10 minutes, then add the tinned tomatoes and cook for another 10 minutes. Separate half the chickpeas with half the cooking water and set aside. Blend the other half of the chickpeas in the remaining cooking water and mix into the vegetables. Cook the soup for about 30 minutes, then add salt, white pepper and nutmeg to taste. Reblend the soup with an immersion blender or jug blender, then add the whole chickpeas in cooking water, and cook for a final 15 minutes. Cut some bread into ¾in/2cm cubes and toast them in the oven. Serve the soup hot with the croutons, a drizzle of extra-virgin olive oil and a sprinkling of fresh ground pepper. As a variation, add 10½ oz/300 g of roughly chopped chard leaves to the soup when you add the whole chickpeas for the final 15 minutes cooking time. This chickpea soup is both delicate and robust at the same time.

Pappa al Pomodoro, Florence Style

INGREDIENTS

35 oz/1 kg of stale bread
about 4 days old
17½ oz/500 g organic
tinned tomatoes, chopped or
blended
3½ oz/100 g onion
30 medium basil leaves
vegetable stock no.3 (page 71)
6 tablespoons extra-virgin olive
oil
black pepper
salt

Serves 5

Cut the bread into 1½in/4cm cubes. Slice the onion as thinly as you can, then fry it in olive oil in a terracotta pot or casserole. After 10 minutes add the tomatoes and the basil leaves and continue cooking for 15 minutes. Add the bread, stir well and cook for another 20 minutes. It will be quite thick so add some vegetable stock no.3 as needed, and add salt and pepper to taste. You might also want to add a pinch of brown sugar to remove the acidity of the tomato. When the bread is soft, serve your hot pappa al pomodoro in soup bowls, with a drizzle of extra-virgin olive oil and a sprinkling of black pepper. A grating of hard salted ricotta cheese is also good. A simple variation on this recipe, but one which completely changes it, is to use 3 large cloves of garlic, cut in half, instead of the onion. This is a popular Tuscan dish, but not all restaurants necessarily have an excellent pappa al pomodoro on their menu. I wanted to give you the two options, onion or garlic, also because there seem to be more and more people with garlic intolerance, so this way we can keep everybody happy. Personally, I like both versions.

Simple recipe from the farming tradition, with strong impact on the senses.

Simple food, costs little, but is always appreciated by adults and children.

Garmugia or Marmugia

INGREDIENTS

3 oz/80 g baby onions
1½ oz/40 g bacon
4½ oz/120 g veal mince
3 medium artichokes
3½ oz/100 g fresh shelled
   peas
3½ oz/100 g fresh shelled
   broad beans
3 oz/80 g asparagus,
   vegetable stock no.1
   (page 70)
slices of toasted crusty bread
5 tablespoons extra-virgin
   olive oil
salt and black pepper

Serves 5

Slice the onions very thinly and fry them gently in extra-virgin olive oil. When they have softened add the bacon diced into small cubes and the veal mince. Fry for about 10 minutes then add all the vegetables – artichokes (remove all the hard external leaves, thorns, and the hairs inside the artichoke heart), broad beans, peas and asparagus and stir for about 5 minutes to mix everything well. Add 2½ pints/2 litres of vegetable stock no.1, and cook for about 30 minutes, then add salt and pepper to taste. Serve piping hot with slices of toasted crusty bread.

Garmugia is made only in the spring in Tuscany, using fresh vegetables, not frozen, and I guarantee you that its freshness is sublime. In the Lucca area there is also a traditional 13th century recipe for this soup in a vegetarian version, without meat. It's known as Marmugia and is also very good.

Tuscan spelt soup

INGREDIENTS

17½ oz/500 g dried organic
   borlotti beans and red beans
20 sage leaves and 5
   unpeeled garlic cloves for
   cooking the beans
25 oz/700 g pearled spelt
3½ oz/100 g onion
3 oz/80 g celery
3 oz/80 g carrot
3 large cloves garlic
2 sprigs rosemary
   8in/20cm long
20 large sage leaves
2 cloves
1 small piece cinnamon stick
8 tablespoons extra-virgin
   olive oil
3½ oz/100 g organic tinned
   tomatoes
white pepper, nutmeg, salt

Serves 10

Soak the beans for at least 12 hours or overnight in cold water. The next day, boil them in 8½ pints/4 litres of lightly salted water with the sage leaves and unpeeled garlic cloves, for about 1½ hours. Chop the celery, carrot, onion, garlic, sage and rosemary very finely, and fry in extra-virgin olive oil for at least 10 minutes, then add the tomatoes, cloves and cinnamon and continue cooking for another 15 minutes. Add half the beans with half their cooking water, stir and cook for 20 minutes and then blend the soup, or better yet put it through a foodmill to purèe it. Rinse the spelt in cold water, add it to the soup along with the remaining whole beans and cooking water, stir everything well and then simmer for about 25 minutes. Add salt, pepper and nutmeg to taste, then let the soup rest for 10 minutes. As usual, if the soup needs to be lengthened with more liquid, use one of our vegetable stocks.

This robust and timeless soup, made with an ancient grain dating from the Roman era, is nutritious and well balanced.

All I can say is, the art of cooking is truly marvellous.

Carabaccia Onion Soup

INGREDIENTS

45 oz/1.3 kg Certaldo
  red onions

8 oz/230 g blanched almonds

2½ pint/1.5 litres vegetable
  stock no.5 (page 72)

9 tablespoons extra-virgin
  olive oil

1 teaspoon icing sugar

1 teaspoon ground cinnamon

salt

Serves 10

Slice the onions very thinly and fry them gently in a pot in extra-virgin olive oil for about 30 minutes. Chop the almonds very finely and mix them into the onions. Then add 2½ pints/2 litres of vegetable stock no.5 (the stock with the flame-seared onion) and continue cooking over a medium-low heat for about 1 hour. When the stock has reduced and the onions are beginning to dissolve, add the teaspoon of sugar and one of cinnamon powder, and then salt to taste. Stir the soup thoroughly to incorporate these last ingredients properly. Carabaccia onion soup should be served hot with ½in/1cm croutons fried in a little butter. This is a historic recipe, and an elegant soup for onion-lovers. It is very delicate and quite special.

Spelt Soup, Maremma Style

INGREDIENTS

9 oz/250 g Tuscan
    pearled spelt

2½ oz/60 g onion

3½ oz/100 g leeks

53 oz/1.5 kg floury potatoes

3½ oz/100 g organic tinned
    tomatoes

5 tablespoons extra-virgin
    olive oil

salt and white pepper

vegetable stock no.1 (page 70)

Serves 5

Chop the onion and leek very finely, and fry in extra-virgin olive oil until softened. Push the tomatoes through a sieve and add to the vegetables, then cook for another 15 minutes. Peel the potatoes and cut into 1¼in/3cm cubes. Add them to the pot, pour in about 2½ pints/2 litres of water and cook for 20 minutes. Add the pearled spelt, and cook for another 30 minutes over a medium heat. The soup should now be quite thick, and some of the potatoes will dissolve during cooking, giving it a pleasing and creamy texture. Add salt and black pepper to taste. Serve the soup hot with a drizzle of extra-virgin olive oil and a sprinkling of freshly ground black pepper. This basic recipe also works very well with brown rice, barley and wheat grains.

The Maremma is a beautiful and very wild natural area in the mid-south of Tuscany, stretching from Castagneto Carducci to Capalbio on the border with Lazio.

Farinata

INGREDIENTS

17½ oz/500 g dried organic
   borlotti beans
7 cloves garlic and 30 sage
   leaves for cooking the beans
25 oz/700 g of Tuscan kale
   or black cabbage
20 oz/600 g corn polenta
   ('ottofile' if possible)
extra-virgin olive oil
salt and black pepper

Serves 10

Soak the beans for at least 12 hours or overnight in cold water. The next day, boil them in 6¼ pints/3 litres of lightly salted water, with 7 cloves of garlic and 30 sage leaves, for about 1½ hours. Wash the kale and cut out the hard central stems. Once the beans are cooked, take half of them out of the cooking water and mash them by pushing them through a foodmill, or use an electric blender. Stir the mashed beans back into the bean soup, add the kale leaves and cook for 30 minutes. Sprinkle the polenta gradually into the soup, stirring all the time, and keep stirring until it is cooked – this depends on the type of polenta used, but usually takes about 30 minutes. To make things easier you could use a top quality precooked polenta. When it is cooked, add salt and pepper to taste and serve the hot soup in terracotta bowls, with a drizzle of extra-virgin olive oil and a sprinkling of freshly ground black pepper. The consistency of the finished farinata is up to you, but it should be fairly thick and solid. Here's a wonderful way to vary the recipe – smear a casserole dish with extra-virgin olive oil, pour the farinata into it and leave to cool, then put it in the fridge. The next day, cut it into 1½in/4cm chunks and put them in the oven at 200°C/400°F for 20 minutes, or fry the chunks in olive oil and serve hot.

Farinata is typically a hot winter dish, but can also be served warm practically all year round. Ottofile is an heirloom varietal of corn, similar to the first corn that arrived in Europe from the Americas. It is still grown in the Garfagnana and midvalley areas of the Serchio river, north of Lucca. This is a grand old recipe, very popular in the areas around Lucca and Arezzo. Polenta with beans and vegetables in some form is very traditional in Tuscany. And it's a delicious combination.

Frantoiana soup

INGREDIENTS

17½ oz/500 g of red beans
  and borlotti beans
25 sage leaves and 5 cloves
  garlic for cooking the beans
2 oz/50 g celery
2 oz/50 g carrot
2 oz/50 g onion, 2 cloves garlic
3½ oz/100 g mixed field
  greens, borage, wild chicory
7 oz/200 g Tuscan kale or
  black cabbage
7 oz/200 g Savoy cabbage,
3½ oz/100 g pumpkin
3½ oz/100 g chard leaves
2 medium onions
3 medium potatoes
3 medium carrots
3 light green zucchinis (courgettes)
2 tablespoons concentrated
  tomato paste
fresh thyme, white pepper, nutmeg
2 cloves, 1 small piece cinnamon
bouquet of sage, rosemary and
  bay leaves
10 tablespoons extra-virgin
  olive oil
salt

10 large slices of toasted bread

Serves 10

Soak the beans in cold water for at least 12 hours or overnight. The next day, cook the beans in 6¼ pints/3 litres of lightly salted water with 25 sage leaves and 5 cloves unpeeled garlic for about 1.5 hours. Chop the celery, carrot, onion and garlic very finely and fry gently in extra-virgin olive oil for 15 minutes along with the cloves and cinnamon. Chop the rest of the vegetables into 1¼in/3cm pieces and add to the pot, then dilute the tomato paste in a little of the beans' cooking water and stir through the vegetables. Using a foodmill or a blender, mash half the beans in half the cooking water and add to the pot along with the bouquet of sage, rosemary and bay leaves. Stir everything well together and simmer for at least 2 hours over a medium heat. At the end of this cooking time, add the fresh thyme and the remaining whole beans with their water, then add salt, white pepper and nutmeg to taste.

In my experience, a frantoiana soup should cook for at least 3 hours total. I remember how, many years ago when I worked in restaurants, people who said they didn't like soup would completely change their opinions and often change their own orders after tasting a dining companion's frantoiana soup.

Serve it hot, drizzled with extra-virgin olive oil and sprinkled with freshly ground black pepper, with toasted garlic-rubbed bread as an accompaniment. My opinion is that this soup is the most important soup in Tuscan culinary culture. There are many different versions, but this is the best one in my experience, and I am very fond of it. Cooking this soup is a spiritual experience, a union of tasty ingredients in poetry and beauty.

Ribollita

INGREDIENTS

17½ oz/500 g dried
  cannellini beans

7 cloves garlic and 20 sage
  leaves for cooking the beans

3½ oz/100 g onion

2 sticks celery

2 carrots

2 cloves garlic

1 sprig rosemary
  4in/10cm long

5 sage leaves

17½ oz/500 g Tuscan kale
  or black cabbage

25 oz/700 g Savoy cabbage

9 oz/250 g chard leaves

3 large potatoes

3 large carrots

2 onions

9 oz/250 g organic tinned
  tomatoes or 1 tablespoon
  concentrated tomato paste

8 tablespoons extra-virgin
  olive oil

fresh thyme

black pepper

salt

25 oz/700 g stale crusty bread

Serves 10

Soak the cannellini beans in cold water for at least 12 hours or overnight. The next day, boil the beans in 6¼ pints/3 litres of water with 7 unpeeled garlic cloves and 20 sage leaves for 1.5 hours. Remove ¼ of the beans, set aside, and mash the remainder in the cooking water using a foodmill or blender. Chop the onion, celery, carrots, garlic, sage and rosemary very finely and fry gently in extra-virgin olive oil for about 10 minutes together with a little fresh thyme. Roughly chop the kale, cabbage and chard. Chop the potatoes, carrots and onions into 1¼in/3cm cubes. Add all the vegetables to the pot, add the tinned tomatoes, mix everything together thoroughly and cook for 10 minutes. Pour the blended bean broth into the pot, and simmer the soup for at least 1 hour. As always, have some vegetable stock on hand to lengthen the soup if necessary. Add the whole cannellini beans that had been set aside, and continue simmering until the soup has a pleasing consistency. Add salt and black pepper to taste. Cut the stale bread into slices, immerge them in the soup and leave it to rest overnight. The next day, gently reheat the soup over a low heat, and serve this extraordinary dish hot or warm with a drizzle of extra-virgin olive oil and some freshly ground black pepper. If there's any left over, it will be even more delicious the following day when it reaches its fullest potential.

Risotti

Porcini Mushroom and Nepitella Risotto

INGREDIENTS

14 oz/400 g Arborio,
  Carnaroli or Vialone rice
2½ oz/60 g onion
5 oz/150 g dried porcini
  mushrooms
2 cloves garlic
30 leaves nepitella
vegetable stock no.5 (page 72)
9 tablespoons of extra-virgin
  olive oil
salt and black pepper

Serves 5

Soak the dried porcini mushrooms in warm water for about 20 minutes. Drain them, rinse thoroughly to eliminate any earth or impurities, then squeeze them out well by hand. Fry the 2 garlic cloves whole in 3 tablespoons of extra-virgin olive oil, then add the mushrooms. Fry gently for about 15 minutes, then remove the garlic cloves. Chop the onion very finely and fry it in a wide pan in 6 tablespoons of extra-virgin olive oil until it has softened, then add the mushrooms and the rice. Stir well and toast the rice for 5 minutes. Add enough vegetable stock no.5 to cover, then stir and continue cooking until the stock is absorbed. Add the nepitella leaves and proceed with cooking the risotto, adding more vegetable stock little by little as it is absorbed into the rice. After 15 minutes, add a little salt and black pepper to taste. When the rice is cooked, take it off the heat, stir well and leave to rest for 2 minutes before serving. It's best not to add parmesan cheese to a porcini mushroom risotto.

Note: Nepitella (Calamintha Nepeta, or Calamint) is a member of the Mint family and is used fresh in Tuscan cuisine, particularly in dishes containing zucchinis or mushrooms. It grows wild in Tuscany, and smells like a cross between mint and oregano. It can be substituted with fresh marjoram, but do not try to use other members of the mint family (spearmint or peppermint) as they have a very different and much stronger pure mint taste than nepitella.

Pescia Asparagus and Saffron Risotto

INGREDIENTS

12½ oz/350 g Arborio,
   Carnaroli or Vialone rice
12½ oz/350 g asparagus
3 oz/80 g onion
6 tablespoons extra-virgin
   olive oil
3 sachets saffron, 0.2 g each
2½ oz/60 g Parmesan cheese
vegetable stock no.1 (page 70)
salt and white pepper

Serves 5

Chop the onion very finely and fry it gently in olive oil in a wide pan for 5 minutes. Wash and dry the asparagus, chop it into 5mm discs and add it to the onion. Fry for another 5 minutes. Then add a little vegetable stock and cook for another 5 minutes until the stock has been absorbed. Add the rice, stir well to amalgamate with the asparagus, and cook for 5 minutes on a medium heat, stirring occasionally, to toast the rice. Pour in enough vegetable stock no.1 to cover the rice, stir and continue cooking, adding the vegetable stock little by little as it is absorbed. The total cooking time for the rice is usually around 20 minutes, depending on the type you use. 5 minutes before the end of cooking time, dissolve the saffron in a cup of vegetable stock and add to the risotto, along with salt and white pepper to taste. When the rice is cooked, take it off the heat, stir in the Parmesan cheese and leave it to rest for a minute. The risotto should be smooth and creamy, delicious and vibrant.

Pescia aparagus is highly appreciated by Italian cooking academies and schools. Pescia, which is also known for its flower-growing industry, is a town in the province of Pistoia, near the small town of Collodi where the legendary story of Pinocchio was born.

Zucchini Flower, Shrimp and Brandy Risotto

INGREDIENTS

14 oz/400 g Arborio,
   Carnaroli or Vialone rice

14 oz/400 g small shrimps
   (prawns)

4 medium-sized zucchinis
   (courgettes)

6 zucchini flowers

1 small bunch parsley

2 cloves garlic

½ chilli pepper

1 fl oz/40 ml brandy

fish stock no.6 (page 73)

6 tablespoons extra-virgin
   olive oil

salt

Serves 5

Chop the zucchinis into small cubes and the flowers into julienne strips and set aside. Chop a little of the parsley very finely with 1 clove of garlic and the chilli pepper, and fry in a wide pan in 2 tablespoons of extra-virgin olive oil for about 1 minute. Add the chopped zucchinis and flowers, stir, then add a little stock and cook for at least 10 minutes. Meanwhile heat the remaining olive oil in a frying pan and fry the other clove of garlic, whole, with the rest of the chopped parsley, for 1 minute. Add the shrimps, pour over the brandy, and sautè quickly on a high heat for just 3 minutes. Add the rice to the zucchinis, stir well to coat the rice and then toast it for a few minutes. Cover the rice with fish stock no.6 and continue cooking, adding stock little by little as it is absorbed. 5 minutes before the end of the rice cooking time, add salt to taste and then stir in the shrimps with their brandy sauce. Finish cooking, then take the risotto off the heat, stir again until it is creamy, and leave to rest for a few minutes. The shrimps shouldn't be cooked too long, no more than 10 minutes total cooking time, or they will become hard. Serve this risotto hot, accompanied by a chilled Vermentino white wine.

Cinta Senese Sausage and Olive Risotto

INGREDIENTS

14 oz/400 g Arborio,
    Carnaroli or Vialone rice
5 oz/150 g Tuscan
    Taggiasche olives, or
    Kalamata olives
10½ oz/300 g Cinta Senese
    sausage
2½ oz/60 g onion
1 medium clove garlic
30 medium basil leaves
7 fl oz/200ml Vernaccia
    di San Gimignano dry
    white wine
4 tablespoons extra-virgin
    olive oil
vegetable stock no.2 (page 70)

Serves 5

Chop the onion and garlic very finely and fry gently in a wide pan in a little olive oil for 5 minutes. Squeeze the sausage meat out of its casing and fry it in another pan with 3 tablespoons of extra-virgin olive oil. Break the sausage meat up with a wooden spoon as it cooks, until it has the texture of minced meat. Pour away the fat that comes out of the sausage meat, then add it to the onion and garlic pan and stir well. Add the rice and stir well again to combine everything. Fry for another 5 minutes to toast the rice then pour over the white wine and evaporate it a little. Cover the rice with vegetable stock and continue cooking until all the wine has evaporated (when there is no more smell of alcohol), at which point add the basil leaves and the olives. Continue cooking, adding more stock little by little as it is absorbed into the rice. When the risotto is cooked, take it off the heat and stir well until it is smooth and creamy. It is important to note that this recipe contains no salt or pepper, because the olives release a lot of salt into the risotto and the Cinta Senese sausage already contains a lot of black pepper. I would also advise you to put very little salt in the vegetable stock when you are preparing it for this particular recipe. You can always add a little more salt if necessary, but you can't take it back out!

The Cinta Senese pig is a Tuscan breed, quite unique for being gray-black, an indigenous and protected species. 20 years ago it was in danger of extinction, but today it is farmed all over Tuscany, although the major area of Cinta Senese farming is the Montagnola Senese.

Etruscan Coast Seafood Risotto

INGREDIENTS

14 oz/400 g Arborio,
   Carnaroli or Vialone rice
35 oz/1 kg clams (ideally
   'vongole veraci' or
   grooved carpet shell
   clams)
1 clove garlic
1 small chilli pepper
10 fresh scampi
10½ oz/300 g green
   beans
3½ oz/100 g Certaldo
   red onion
10 cherry tomatoes
1 small bunch parsley
5 fl oz/150 ml dry
   white wine
12 tablespoons extra-
   virgin olive oil
shellfish stock no.7
   (page 73)
salt and white pepper

Serves 5

Make the stock no. 7 using the scampi heads. Cut the tails in half and set aside. Put the clams in cold water with a pinch of salt for about 1 hour, then tap them one by one against a hard surface, to check for any sand inside. Cut the cherry tomatoes into quarters and set aside. Cut the green beans into ¾in/2cm pieces and cook in lightly salted water for about 10 minutes then drain. Chop the onion very finely and fry it in 4 tablespoons of extra-virgin olive oil until it starts to soften, then add the green beans and a pinch of white pepper, and sauté for 4 minutes. Chop the garlic, chilli pepper and parsley very finely. Keep 2 teaspoons of chopped parsley aside to complete the dish at the end, and fry the rest with the garlic and chilli pepper in another pan, in 4 tablespoons of extra-virgin olive oil, for about 2 minutes. Add the clams and cover the pan. When the clams have opened a little, pour the white wine over them and cook for about 5 minutes.

Now we are ready to assemble our risotto! Heat the remaining 4 tablespoons of olive oil in a wide pan which you will use to cook the risotto. Add the rice, stir to coat well with the oil and toast it for a few minutes. Cover the rice with the shellfish stock and continue cooking, adding stock little by little as it gets absorbed into the rice. 5 minutes before the end of cooking time, add the hot ingredients (the clams with their cooking liquid, the onion and green bean mixture), and finally the scampi tails. When the rice is cooked, take it off the heat and stir in the quartered cherry tomatoes and the remaining 2 teaspoons of chopped parsley. Stir for a few minutes until the risotto is smooth and creamy, then add salt and pepper to taste, and serve this splendid seafood risotto hot and cooked 'al dente'. I have modified this recipe over time, and I really like its vibrant and striking tones. The Etruscan coast stretches from Donoratico to the Gulf of Baratti in the province of Livorno. These are magical and timeless places, one of the many wonders of Tuscany, where the ancient Etruscans fished the waters and farmed the land by the sea.

Artichoke and Turmeric Risotto, Empoli Style

INGREDIENTS

14 oz/400 g Arborio,
  Carnaroli or Vialone rice
10 purple artichokes
juice of 1 lemon
2½ oz/60 g onion
1 small bunch parsley
1 teaspoon turmeric
6 tablespoons extra-virgin
  olive oil
vegetable stock no.5 (page 72)
salt and white pepper

Serves 5

Clean the artichokes – remove the hard external leaves, cut off all the thorns and remove the hairs from inside the artichoke heart. Cut each artichoke heart into 8 pieces, and put in cold water with the lemon juice. Chop the onion and parsley very finely and fry in a wide pan in the extra-virgin olive oil for 4 minutes. Drain the artichokes, rinse them, add them to the onion and fry for at least 10 minutes. Add the rice and stir well to mix with the artichokes, then toast it for about 4 minutes. Cover the rice with vegetable stock no.5 and continue cooking, adding more stock as it is absorbed by the risotto. 5 minutes before the end of cooking time, add the turmeric, salt and white pepper. When the rice is cooked, take it off the heat and stir the risotto for about 2 minutes. There is no need to add butter if the rice is of excellent quality, as the starch in the rice will give the risotto a pleasing and creamy consistency.

The original recipe only contains artichokes, but I like to add turmeric which is a wonderful spice with many health-benefitting properties. This recipe comes from Empoli, a town which is well-known for the cultivation of top-quality artichokes.

Dried Pasta

Spaghetti With Cherry Tomatoes, Zucchinis, Basil and Pine Nuts

INGREDIENTS

17½ oz/500 g top quality
   spaghetti
(bronze-extruded, from
   Gragnano if possible)
28 oz/800 g cherry tomatoes
3 oz/80 g pine nuts
4 medium zucchinis (courgettes)
2 cloves garlic
30 basil leaves
7 tablespoons extra-virgin
   olive oil
salt and black pepper
(optional sprinkling of
   Parmesan cheese)

Serves 5

Slice the garlic thinly, quarter the zucchinis lengthwise, and then slice very thinly. Fry the garlic and pine nuts in extra-virgin olive oil for a couple of minutes. Add the sliced zucchinis and cook on a high heat for about 10 minutes. Chop the tomatoes in half and add to the pan along with the basil leaves torn in half. Add salt and 5 twists of the pepper mill. Cook for another 5 minutes over a high heat, adding a little of the pasta cooking water to ensure the sauce doesn't dry up too much. The fresh sweet tomatoes give the sauce a pleasingly creamy consistency. Cook the spaghetti 'al dente' in abundant boiling salted water and drain them 3 minutes before the end of cooking time. Finish cooking the spaghetti in the pan with the sauce, again adding pasta cooking water as necessary. Serve garnished with a basil leaf.

This is a simple and tasty recipe, good for every occasion, quick to make yet impressive. The secret is to use top quality bronze-extruded pasta, preferably from the Gragnano area of Naples.

Linguine with Seafood and Zucchinis

INGREDIENTS

17½ oz/500 g top quality
  linguine pasta (bronze-
  extruded, from Gragnano
  if possible)

17½ oz/500 g mussels

28 oz/800 g clams

5 oz/150 g pale zucchinis
  (courgettes)

20 leaves nepitella

4 teaspoons chopped parsley

2 medium cloves garlic

1 small dried chilli pepper

7 fl oz/200ml dry white wine

10 tablespoons extra-virgin
  olive oil, salt

Serves 5

Rinse the mussels, scrub them and remove any beards. Soak the clams for an hour in a bowl of cold water with a pinch of salt, then tap them one by one against a hard surface to make sure there is no sand inside. Chop the garlic and chilli pepper very finely. Put 3 tablespoons of extra-virgin olive oil in each of 2 large frying pans, and divide the garlic and chilli pepper mix between them. Fry for about 1 minute and then put the mussels in one pan and the clams in the other. Pour 3¼ fl oz/100 ml of white wine in each pan, cover both and cook for 8 minutes until the shellfish start to open. Don't overcook them or they will become hard. Check there is no sand in the clams' cooking liquid, filter it to be sure. Mix the mussels and clams together in one of the pans along with their cooking liquids. Cut the zucchinis in half lengthways and then slice them thinly into half-moon shapes. Fry the zucchinis for 5 minutes in another pan with the remaining 4 tablespoons of olive oil, a pinch of salt and the nepitella leaves. Mix the zucchinis with the mussels and clams, and stir in the chopped parsley. Cook the linguine in abundant boiling salted water and drain 3 minutes before the end of cooking time. Finish cooking the pasta in the pan with the shellfish and zucchinis, adding a little of the pasta cooking water if necessary. The sauce should be creamy, serve the pasta piping hot and cooked 'al dente'.

This is a classic Italian recipe from the Tuscan coast, and there are an infinite number of variations which we will investigate in future books. For now, this is one of my favourites, because of the zucchinis. I really like to add vegetables to fish recipes – they make the recipe much more nutritious. You can also try this recipe with normal spaghetti or hand-made spaghetti cut on a pasta guitar.

Rigatoni With Asparagus, Cherry Tomatoes and Flaked Almonds

INGREDIENTS

17½ oz/500 g top quality
  rigatoni pasta (bronze-
  extruded, from Gragnano if
  possible)
25 oz/700 g Piccadilly or
  cherry tomatoes
2 oz/50 g onion
2 large cloves garlic
12½ oz/350 g asparagus
3 oz/80 g almond flakes
1 small bunch parsley
7 tablespoons extra-virgin olive
  oil
salt and white pepper
(optional sprinkling of Pecorino
  Romano cheese)

Serves 5

Slice the asparagus thinly, leaving the tips whole. Chop the garlic and the onion very finely, and fry in extra-virgin olive oil for about 3 minutes. Add the asparagus and cook on a high heat for 10 minutes, adding some of the pasta cooking water as needed. Quarter the tomatoes and add them to the pan, with the flaked almonds. Cook for another 5 minutes or until the tomatoes have softened and released their juice. Add salt and pepper to taste, and two pinches of chopped parsley. Cook your rigatoni in salted water until 'al dente' and drain 3 minutes prior to the end of cooking time, reserving some of the cooking water. Finish cooking the pasta in the pan with the asparagus sauce, adding a little cooking water as needed. Serve your rigatoni hot with a drizzle of olive oil and an optional sprinkling of Pecorino Romano cheese. For lovers of asparagus, this is the perfect dish.

Pici or Spaghetti With Cheese and Pepper or "Cacio E Pepe"

INGREDIENTS

17½ oz/500 g dried pici
    pasta or thick spaghetti
14 oz/400 g grated Pecorino
    Romano or mature Crete
    Senesi pecorino cheese
fresh ground black pepper,
salt

Serves 5

Cook your pici or spaghetti in boiling salted water. While the pasta is cooking, ladle out the cooking water and put it in a separate saucepan on a low heat. Continue cooking the pasta in very little water, adding back the cooking water a little at a time, as though it were stock and you were cooking a risotto. One minute before the pasta is fully cooked, take the pan off the heat, add the grated cheese and about 30 twists of the pepper mill. Stir vigorously so the cheese does not form strings. It's very important that the pasta stays 'al dente', and the sauce should be smooth and creamy. Serve piping hot with an additional sprinkling of grated cheese and black pepper. This recipe is typically Roman when made with bucatini pasta, but it can also be found in many restaurants in the Siena area, made with pici pasta instead. I wanted to include this recipe because it is so simple but tastes so good. It is also one of the very few recipes in this book that do not require olive oil.

Tuscan Gigli with Seared Vegetables

INGREDIENTS

17½ oz/500 g Tuscan
   gigli pasta
5 oz/150 g red onion,
5 oz/150 g carrot
7 oz/200 g zucchinis
   (courgettes)
3½ oz/100 g celery
5 oz/150 g eggplant
   (aubergine)
25 basil leaves
15 cherry tomatoes
7 tablespoons extra-virgin
   olive oil
salt and white pepper

Serves 5

Gigli is a cone-shaped type of pasta which looks like a small flower, more specifically a lily. Chop the red onion, carrots, zucchinis, celery and eggplant into ½in/1cm cubes. Put the olive oil in a pan and heat it on a high heat for about 2 minutes. Add the vegetable cubes. Cook for about 8 minutes on a high heat, then add salt and pepper to taste. Add the cherry tomatoes (quartered) and the basil leaves (torn in half). Continue cooking for another 2 minutes then take the pan off the heat.

Cook your Tuscan gigli in abundant boiling salted water, drain and toss for about a minute in the pan with the vegetables, adding a little of the pasta cooking water as needed. Serve hot with an optional sprinkling of Parmesan cheese. It's a quick and easy recipe, fresh-tasting and suitable for all occasions.

The lily is the flower symbol of Tuscany, so it is particularly appropriate, but you can do this recipe with any short type of pasta such as fusilli or penne etc.

Pasta in Fresh Tomato Sauce or "Pommarola"

INGREDIENTS

17½ oz/500 g top quality
   pasta, long or short shape
   (bronze-extruded if possible)
3½ oz/100 g celery,
3½ oz/100 g carrot
3½ oz/100 g onion,
6 vine tomatoes
25 medium basil leaves
8 tablespoons extra-virgin
   olive oil
25 oz/700 g organic tinned
   peeled tomatoes
2 pinches organic brown sugar
¾ oz/20 g salt, (optional
   sprinkling of Parmesan or
   Pecorino Romano cheeses)

Chop the celery, carrot and onion into ½in/1cm pieces. Cut the vine tomatoes into quarters. Put all the ingredients into a saucepan – tinned tomatoes, celery, carrot, onion, basil leaves, vine tomatoes, extra-virgin olive oil, salt and brown sugar. Cook on a medium heat for about 40 minutes. Allow to cool a little then put the sauce through a foodmill to purèe it. It is best not to use an electric blender, because it tends to change the look of the sauce, making it lighter. Instead of rich tomato red it will become orange, and that's not what we want. Put the sauce back on a low heat for another 20 minutes, at which point you should start to see the oil floating to the surface of the sauce, and when this happens, it is ready. Cook your pasta in plenty of boiling salted water, drain it 2 minutes before the end of cooking time and finish cooking with the fresh pommarola sauce. Serve the pasta piping hot with an optional sprinkling of Parmesan or Pecorino Romano cheeses.

This is also a classic Italian recipe that has many variations, but this version is my favourite. Use the best quality organic tinned tomatoes that you can find, as they will have a lower level of acidity. You can also use tinned cherry tomatoes which are a little sweeter. In Tuscany this sauce is also called 'fake' sauce, because the basis of the recipe is the same as for a meat ragù, and it is cooked for a long time like a ragù, but there is no meat in it.

An excellent every-day recipe, fresh and nutritious, and everyone likes it.

Fresh Pasta

Tagliolini with San Miniato White Truffle

INGREDIENTS

14 oz/400 g fresh egg
   tagliolini pasta
3½ oz/100 g butter
3 oz/80 g San Miniato white
   trufflea few tablespoons of
   the pasta cooking water
1 pinch salt
for the pasta:
3 large eggs
10½ oz/300 g 0 grade flour
or plain all-purpose flour
4 tablespoons warm water
2 teaspoons extra-virgin olive oil
1 pinch salt

Serves 5

BASIC RECIPE FOR FRESH EGG PASTA

Make a crater with the flour – I like to call it a volcano – and break
the eggs into it. Add the water, extra-virgin olive oil and a pinch
of salt. Using a fork, whisk the eggs in the middle of the crater,
and when they are completely blended keep whisking but start to
incorporate the flour little by little from around the rim of the crater
until you have a soft dough. At first the dough will be very soft and
sticky, so use a spatula to lift and incorporate any pieces that stick to
the work surface and carry on kneading the dough by hand until it is
smooth and elastic. The dough is ready when you press a finger into
it and it slowly springs back. Let it rest for at least 15 minutes so that it
becomes even more elastic. Roll it out quite thin using a rolling pin or
pasta machine. Flour the sheet of pasta, fold it into thirds and then cut
it into 2mm wide strips, cutting across from one of the folded edges.
Lift and shake out the strips which are now 'tagliolini'. Sprinkle them
with fine-ground durum wheat semolina to stop them from sticking.
Cook the tagliolini in boiling salted water for about 3 minutes. Melt
the butter in a frying pan and add a few tablespoons of the pasta
cooking water. Drain the pasta, then put it in the pan with the butter
and toss until the tagliolini are creamy and well coated with butter.
Pile the hot pasta on a serving dish and grate the white truffle on top.
In Italy the most important areas for white truffles are Alba in Piedmont
and San Miniato in Tuscany. The small medieval town of San Miniato
is in the province of Pisa, and every year in November it hosts a
famous truffle festival which attracts thousands of hungry visitors from
all over the world. For truffle-lovers, this is a classic and divine recipe.
We can also use truffle oil instead of butter in this recipe.

Tagliolini in Black Truffle Sauce

INGREDIENTS

2 medium cloves garlic

7 fl oz/200 ml extra-virgin
  olive oil

7 oz/200 g fresh black truffle

FOR THE PASTA

3 large eggs

10½ oz/300 g 0 grade flour
  or plain all-purpose flour

4 tablespoons warm water

2 teaspoons extra-virgin olive oil

1 pinch of salt

Serves 5

Make the tagliolini using the method in the previous recipe. For the sauce, put the extra-virgin olive oil in a saucepan with 2 peeled cloves of garlic and heat until the garlic begins to fry. Take the pan off the heat immediately and grate the black truffle into it. The truffle aroma will be very intense, but be careful not to overheat the oil or you will end up with burnt garlic and burnt truffle. Remove the garlic cloves. Cook the tagliolini pasta in boiling salted water for about 3 minutes, drain and dress with the truffle sauce. Serve the pasta hot, in a glass serving dish, accompanied by a good Tuscan red wine.

This recipe originates in the border area between the province of Arezzo in Tuscany and Città di Castello in Umbria. For truffle-lovers, this recipe has to use black truffles, which are expensive but still much cheaper than white ones. Friends in both Tuscany and Umbria advise me to be generous with the amount of truffle used, as the aroma of this sauce is simply unforgettable. Don't add any Parmesan cheese – this dish is about the rich aroma of earth.

Spaghetti "alla Chitarra" with Clams, Asparagus and Shrimps

INGREDIENTS

35 oz/1 kg clams,
5 oz/150 g whole
   shrimps (prawns)
9 oz/250 g asparagus
2 medium cloves garlic
2 oz/50 g onion
3 teaspoons chopped
   parsley
7 fl oz/200ml dry
   white wine
9 tablespoons extra-
   virgin olive oil
1 small dried chilli pepper
shellfish stock no.7
   (page 73)
salt

FOR THE PASTA

3 large eggs
20 oz/600 g 0 grade
   flour or plain all-
   purpose flour
3 tablespoons warm water
3 teaspoons extra-virgin
   olive oil
2 pinches of salt

Serves 5

The method for making the pasta is similar to the previous recipes, but I would advise you to add a little more flour so that the pasta dough is a little firmer than usual. Then roll it out using a rolling pin or pasta machine until it has the same dimensions as your 'chitarra' or pasta guitar, which is what we call the wooden box with metal strings that we use for cutting spaghetti. As the pasta sheet is a little more solid it won't stick to the strings when it is pressed through with a rolling pin. It will separate into spaghetti strings without difficulty. There are many recipes using durum wheat flour for guitar spaghetti, but we will look at these in future books.

For the sauce, we use 'lupin' clams if possible, also known as rayed artemis clams, which are small and delicious, well suited to this recipe. Whatever sort of clams you are using, put them in a bowl of cold water with a pinch of salt. Use the shrimp heads to make the concentrated shellfish stock no.7. Chop the onion very finely and fry it in 4 tablespoons of extra-virgin olive oil for 3 minutes. Slice the asparagus into discs, leaving the tips whole. Add the asparagus to the pan and fry for 10 minutes and then add 2 pinches of salt. Chop the garlic cloves and chilli pepper very finely, mix with the chopped parsley and fry for 1 minute in the remaining olive oil, then add the clams. After 3 minutes pour over the white wine. Add the unpeeled shrimp tails and cook for another 5 minutes. Add the cooked asparagus, a little salt, and mix everything well together.

Cook the spaghetti in abundant boiling salted water for about 4 minutes, drain and mix in the pan with the seafood sauce. Serve piping hot, arranging the spaghetti into nests on the serving plate with the clams, shrimps and asparagus piled inside and around the nests. A drizzle of extra-virgin olive oil and a sprinkling of grated pepper is an extra touch. This is 'cucina bianca' – white, as in no tomato, and the taste and aroma of the sea is extraordinary. You can use this sauce to dress tagliolini, tagliatelle, spaghetti and linguine shapes of pasta. Have fun!

Tagliatelle With Duck Ragù

INGREDIENTS

½ duck, around 28 oz/800 g
2 oz/50 g celery
2½ oz/60 g carrot
2½ oz/60 g onion
1 large clove garlic
2 cloves
1 small piece cinnamon stick
7 tablespoons extra-virgin
  olive oil
1 fresh bay leaf
5 fl oz/150 ml dry white wine
2 oz/50 g organic tinned
  peeled tomatoes
1 teaspoon of chopped parsley
vegetable stock no.5 (page 72)
white pepper
nutmeg, salt

FOR THE PASTA

4 large eggs
14 oz/400 g 0 grade flour or
  plain all-purpose flour
4 tablespoons warm water
2 teaspoons extra-virgin olive oil
1 pinch of salt

Serves 5

Make the pasta dough using the method in the previous recipes. When you roll it out, make it slightly thicker than for the tagliolini, then lightly flour the sheet of pasta, fold it in half and then in half again in the same direction, and cut it into strips ½in/1cm wide, cutting across from the folded edge. Lift and shake out the strips and you have your 'tagliatelle' or ribbons of pasta. Sprinkle them with fine-ground durum wheat semolina to prevent them from sticking together.

For the duck ragù, cut the duck into 2⅜in/6cm pieces, wash and dry them with a cloth. Chop the celery, carrot, onion and garlic very finely and fry in the extra-virgin olive oil along with the bay leaf, cloves and cinnamon for at least 10 minutes until the vegetables have softened. Add the duck pieces and brown them on all sides. Pour over the wine and then add enough vegetable stock no.5 to cover everything. Simmer until the wine has evaporated and there is no more smell of alcohol. Break the tomatoes into pieces by hand and add them to the sauce, along with a little salt, pepper, and a sprinkling of grated nutmeg. Simmer on a medium heat for at least an hour, adding more vegetable stock if the sauce thickens too much or starts to stick. Take the pan off the heat and leave to cool. Strip the duck meat from the bones, chop it coarsely with a knife, and put it back in the pan with the sauce. Put the bones in a small pan of vegetable stock and boil for about 10 minutes. Filter this stock, stir it into the sauce and simmer again. When the duck sauce or ragù has reduced to a good creamy consistency, stir in the teaspoon of chopped parsley and it is ready.

Cook your fresh tagliatelle pasta in boiling salted water for about 6 minutes, drain it and mix with the duck ragù until every ribbon of pasta is coated with a generous quantity of this rich sauce. For those who like duck, this dish is really quite delightful. Serve it hot with an optional sprinkling of Parmesan cheese.

Tagliatelle Grosseto Style

INGREDIENTS

20 oz/600 g shrimps (prawns)

35 oz/1 kg mussels

9 oz/250 g baby squid

5 oz/150 g fresh peas
  (exceptionally good in
  spring season)

2 large cloves garlic

1 small dried chilli pepper

7 fl oz/200ml dry white wine

2 tablespoons chopped fresh
  parsley

9 tablespoons extra-virgin
  olive oil

salt and white pepper

FOR THE PASTA

4 large eggs

14 oz/400 g 0 grade flour or
  plain all-purpose flour

4 tablespoons warm water

2 teaspoons extra-virgin olive oil

1 pinch of salt

Serves 5

Make the tagliatelle according to the method given in the previous recipe.

For the sauce, wash and peel the shrimps and use the heads to make a little shellfish stock no.7. Cut the squid into thin strips and scrub the mussels clean, removing the byssal threads or 'beards'. Shell the peas and cook them on their own for 10 minutes in boiling water with a pinch of salt and 2 tablespoons of extra-virgin olive oil. Chop the garlic and chilli pepper very finely, and fry briefly for a minute in the remaining olive oil. Add the squid, fry for 5 minutes and then pour over 3¼ fl oz/100 ml of the wine. The squid cooking time needs to be very brief if they are small and tender, otherwise you will have to cook them for a long time until they soften. Add the mussels and the peeled shrimps, pour over the remaining 3¼ fl oz/100 ml of wine and simmer for 10 minutes. If the sauce dries up too much add a little of the shellfish stock no.7 as needed. Add the drained peas, stir in the chopped parsley and your sauce is ready. Cook the tagliatelle in abundant boiling salted water for about 6 minutes, drain and toss with the sauce. These splendid tagliatelle Grosseto style should be served piping hot. Use fresh peas if possible – this changes the whole sense of the dish, giving it a feeling of intense freshness.

Pappardelle with Rabbit Ragù

INGREDIENTS

½ rabbit, about 25 oz/700 g

2 oz/50 g celery

2½ oz/60 g onion

2½ oz/60 g carrot

1 large clove garlic

2 large sage leaves

1 sprig of rosemary,
   2in/5cm long

1 sprig fresh thyme

7 tablespoons extra-virgin
   olive oil

5 fl oz/150 ml dry white
   wine, 2 fresh bay leaves

3½ oz/100 g organic tinned
   peeled tomatoes

vegetable stock no.5 (page 72)

nutmeg, black pepper. salt

FOR THE PASTA

5 large eggs

17½ oz/500 g 0 grade flour
   or plain all-purpose flour

5 tablespoons warm water

3 teaspoons extra-virgin olive oil

2 pinches of salt

Serves 5

To make the pappardelle, follow the method for tagliatelle in the previous recipes but cut the strips of pasta ¾in/2cm wide.

For the rabbit ragù, cut the rabbit into 2⅜in/6cm pieces and wash and dry them with a cloth. Chop the celery, carrot, onion, garlic, sage, rosemary and thyme very finely, and fry them together in extra-virgin olive oil for about 5 minutes. Add the rabbit pieces to the pan and brown them on all sides. Pour over the wine and then add enough vegetable stock no.5 to cover everything. Simmer on a medium-high heat until the wine has evaporated (there will be no more smell of alcohol), then add the bay leaves and the tomatoes. Cook for about an hour, adding vegetable stock as necessary when the sauce thickens too much. Add a little salt, black pepper and freshly grated nutmeg. Take the pan off the heat, allow to cool, then strip the rabbit meat from the bones and chop it roughly with a knife. Put the bones in a small pan of vegetable stock and boil for about 10 minutes. Filter this stock and add it to the sauce, along with the rabbit meat. Simmer the rabbit sauce or ragù until the liquid reduces again, then add more salt, pepper or nutmeg to taste, and your ragù is ready.

Cook your pappardelle pasta in abundant boiling salted water for about 7 minutes, drain it and mix into the ragù. Toss the pasta in the pan and add a little vegetable stock if necessary – the sauce should be creamy. Serve hot with a sprinkling of Parmesan cheese on top. This dish is both delicate and robust, those who like white meat will particularly appreciate it.

Maccheroni with Tuscan Sausage and Dried Porcini Mushrooms

INGREDIENTS

25 oz/700 g Tuscan
   pork sausage

3 oz/80 g onion

2 medium cloves garlic

4 tablespoons extra-virgin
   olive oil

5 fl oz/150 ml dry white wine

2 oz/50 g dried porcini
   mushrooms

100 organic tinned peeled
   tomatoes

vegetable stock no.5 (page 72)

no salt and no pepper!

FOR THE PASTA

4 large eggs

14 oz/400 g 0 grade flour or
   plain all-purpose flour

4 tablespoons warm water

3 teaspoons extra-virgin olive oil

2 pinches of salt

Serves 5

Make the pasta dough according to the method given in the previous recipes but when you roll it out, using a rolling pin or a pasta machine, make it into a sheet about 2mm thick and then cut it into small squares about 2 x 2in/5 x 5cm. Arrange the squares in rows and layers on a pasta board or work surface and sprinkle them with fine-ground durum wheat semolina so they do not stick to each other. One very important little note: Tuscan maccheroni are these squares of fresh egg pasta, and not tubes of dried pasta as in southern Italy. They are also called tacconi, which means 'big heel', as in the heel of a shoe. Many people, both southern Italians and foreigners, go to restaurants around Lucca and Pisa and order maccheroni, thinking they will get those tubes of pasta, and instead they are always amazed to be served with these flat Tuscan maccheroni.

For the sauce, first put the dried porcini mushrooms to soak in warm water for at least 15 minutes. Meanwhile, chop the onion and garlic very finely and fry in extra-virgin olive oil for at least 5 minutes. Squeeze the sausage meat out of its casing and into the pan, breaking it up first with your hands and then with a wooden spoon as it cooks. When the sausage meat has browned a little, pour over the white wine and add enough vegetable stock no.5 to cover everything. Drain the soaked mushrooms and rinse them well to remove any residues of earth or impurities. When the wine has evaporated (there will be no more smell of alcohol), add the mushrooms and the tomatoes. The sauce must reflect the deep rich shades of the sausage and mushrooms, so it should tend towards brown rather than red. Simmer the sauce on a medium heat for about 1 hour.

Cook the maccheroni in abundant boiling salted water for 5 minutes and then drain. Mix the pasta with the sausage and mushroom sauce, adding a little of the pasta cooking water to make it creamier. You should always keep a little of your pasta cooking water to help amalgamate pasta and sauce in any recipe. There is no salt or pepper in this recipe, because the sausage already contains enough of both. Serve this dish piping hot, with a light sprinkling of Parmesan cheese if desired. This is a mouth-watering and satisfying dish for an autumn Sunday lunch, accompanied by a full-bodied red wine.

Fresh Stuffed Pasta

Ravioli in Tomato Sauce, Lunigiana Style

INGREDIENTS FOR THE FILLING

20 oz/600 g floury potatoes,
17½ oz/500 g fresh chard
   leaves, 2 large eggs
3 oz/80 g Parmesan cheese
3 oz/80 g breadcrumbs
nutmeg, black pepper, salt
Ingredients for the sauce:
14 oz/400 g organic tinned
   peeled tomatoes
2½ oz/60 g celery
3 oz/80 g onion
3 oz/80 g carrot
20 basil leaves
9 tablespoons extra-virgin
   olive oil
2 pinches brown sugar, salt

FOR THE PASTA DOUGH

4 large eggs
17½ oz/500 g 0 grade flour
   or plain flour
4 tablespoons warm water,
3 tablespoons extra-virgin olive
   oil, 2 pinches of salt
Serves 5

PROCEDURE FOR THE FILLING

Cook the unpeeled potatoes in boiling salted water. When you can pierce a potato easily with a fork, they are cooked. Drain them and leave them to cool, then peel and mash them with a fork. Wilt the chard leaves, squeeze out as much water as possible, and chop them finely. Mix the mashed potatoes with the chard, add the eggs, Parmesan cheese, breadcrumbs, white pepper, salt and nutmeg. The filling must be very evenly blended and tasty.

PROCEDURE FOR THE PASTA

Make the pasta dough the same way as described in the previous chapter, Fresh Pasta. This applies to all the fresh stuffed pasta recipes in this chapter. Make the ravioli following the procedure in the previous recipe of this chapter.

Dice the celery, onion and carrot finely and fry in olive oil for at least 5 minutes. Crush the tomatoes into small pieces by hand, then add to the vegetables, along with the basil leaves, sugar and salt. Simmer the sauce gently for 20 minutes. Cook the ravioli in abundant boiling salted water for about 8 minutes. Drain them and dress them with the freshly-cooked tomato sauce. Serve the ravioli piping hot with a drizzle of extra-virgin olive oil, a sprinkling of black pepper and mature Pecorino Romano cheese.

These vegetarian ravioli have a wonderful texture and taste. You can serve them with the same butter sage dressing from the previous recipe, or with a meat ragù, but in my opinion their true destiny in the kitchen is to be smothered in this tomato sauce with pecorino cheese sprinkled on top. You will sense the softness of the vegetables and in this simple delicious recipe with its origins in 'cucina povera' or peasant cooking. The Lunigiana is an area that stretches from the Liguria region to Parma in the Emilia Romagna region, and down to Tuscany, touching Massa and Carrara and the mountains of the Garfagnana area north of Lucca. A fascinating land – full of history and mystery and a rich culinary tradition with wonderful recipes. The Lunigiana is the first port of call on the journey into Tuscan cuisine.

Ravioli Stuffed with Ricotta Cheese, Spinach and Chard, Dressed in Sage Butter and Nutmeg

INGREDIENTS FOR THE FILLING

17½ oz/500 g fresh sheep's
  milk ricotta
17½ oz/500 g fresh spinach
17½ oz/500 g chard leaves
3½ oz/100 g Parmesan cheese
2 eggs
3 oz/80 g breadcrumbs
white pepper, nutmeg, salt

FOR THE PASTA DOUGH

4 large eggs
17½ oz/500 g 0 grade flour
  or plain flour
4 tablespoons warm water
3 teaspoons extra-virgin olive oil
2 pinches of salt

The procedure for the pasta dough is always the same, as in the previous chapter, Fresh Pasta. Roll the dough out using a rolling pin or a pasta machine, and cut it into 4¾in/12cm wide strips. Using two teaspoons, place teaspoonfuls of the filling onto the pasta strips, about 2⅜in/6cm apart, in a line down the centre of the pasta. Fold the pasta over the filling, press the pasta down to seal it in between the lumps of filling, making sure you squeeze out any air because this will expand during cooking and make the ravioli break open. Separate the ravioli by cutting between the filling using a non-serrated knife. Seal the ravioli on 3 sides using a fork. Be careful not to pierce or puncture the pasta too close to the filling. Seal them well – in fact this is the most important part of making ravioli.

PROCEDURE FOR THE FILLING

Wilt the washed spinach and chard leaves in boiling salted water for about 10 minutes. Let them cool and then squeeze out as much water as possible using your hands. Chop the leaves very, very finely – they need to be reduced to a smooth type of pulp without any lumps. Don't use a blender because the power of the blades destroys the fibres in the leaves and they exude more water. Put the spinach and chard pulp in a bowl, add the ricotta and mix well until evenly blended. If you can't find sheep's milk ricotta, use cow's milk ricotta just the same. Add the Parmesan cheese, bread crumbs, eggs, salt, white pepper and nutmeg (to taste), and stir everything together until it is evenly amalgamated. Once you have made the ravioli, cook them in abundant boiling salted water for about 8 minutes. They will

INGREDIENTS FOR THE DRESSING
7 oz/200 g butter

30 medium sage leaves

nutmeg

Serves 5

rise to the surface of the water so use a wooden spoon to stir gently every now and then so they all cook evenly.

PROCEDURE FOR THE DRESSING
Put everything together in a pan – butter, sage and nutmeg – on a low heat until the butter melts. This only takes a few minutes so be careful not to let the butter burn. Drain the ravioli and toss them in a bowl with the sage butter dressing and a little of the ravioli cooking water. Sprinkle with Parmesan cheese and toss again to mix. Serve hot with extra Parmesan cheese on top.

This is one of my all-time favourite dishes – I would place it in my top ten. The ravioli are soft and buttery, and the combination of the ingredients is an extraordinary pleasure for the palate. You could also dress these ravioli with white truffle butter, simple tomato sauce or cherry tomato sauce. They also work well with meat-based sauces.

Ravioli with Ricotta Cheese and Walnuts

INGREDIENTS FOR THE FILLING

20 oz/600 g sheep's milk
   ricotta cheese
7 oz/200 g walnut pieces
3 oz/80 g Parmesan cheese
2½ oz/60 g breadcrumbs
2 large eggs
white pepper, nutmeg, salt

FOR THE PASTA DOUGH

4 large eggs
17½ oz/500 g 0 grade flour
   or plain flour
4 tablespoons warm water
3 teaspoons extra-virgin olive oil
2 pinches of salt

FOR THE SAUCE

25 oz/700 g cherry tomatoes
2 large garlic cloves
8 tablespoons extra-virgin
   olive oil
25 medium basil leaves,
salt and white pepper
grated Pecorino Romano cheese

Serves 5

Make the pasta dough following the usual method, as explained in the previous chapter.

Procedure for the filling: chop the walnuts finely using a knife. Put them in a bowl and add the ricotta cheese, eggs, breadcrumbs, grated Parmesan cheese, salt, white pepper and nutmeg. Mix everything with a fork until it is evenly blended. Make the ravioli following the procedure given in previous recipes.

PROCEDURE FOR THE SAUCE

Wash, dry and quarter the tomatoes. Fry the garlic for 2 minutes in extra-virgin olive oil, then add the tomatoes and fry for another 5 minutes on a high heat. Add salt and white pepper, and the basil leaves. Cook for another 5 minutes and the fresh cherry tomato sauce is ready. Cook your ravioli in abundant boiling salted water for about 8 minutes. Drain them and toss them in the pan with the tomato sauce. Serve piping hot with a sprinkling of grated Pecorino Romano cheese. What a treat!

It's important to use the freshest ricotta and the best walnuts you can obtain. These are the two main ingredients so their quality will make all the difference to the final dish, creating a well-balanced filling and an explosion of delicious tastes in the mouth when you eat the ravioli.

This is a recipe from the rolling Tuscan hillsides – hills which rise up to the mountains where shepherds graze their sheep under walnut trees. I remember when I had my own restaurant and the ricotta cheese would arrive in the morning, freshly made and still warm. It was hard not to eat it all immediately, and as fast as I could make these ravioli people had already ordered them. These are beautiful and emotional memories of this rustic and evocative dish.

Tordelli Lucca Style

INGREDIENTS FOR THE FILLING

25 oz/700 g top quality
  beef mince

3½ oz/100 g air-cured ham

3½ oz/100 g mortadella

14 oz/400 g stale bread,
  soaked in fresh milk

3 eggs

2 oz/50 g parsley

5½ oz/160 g freshly grated
  Parmesan cheese

3 oz/80 g breadcrumbs

4 tablespoons extra-virgin olive
  oil

A few fresh thyme or
  'pepolino' leaves

black pepper, nutmeg, salt

FOR THE PASTA

10 large eggs

35 oz/1 kg 0 grade flour or
  plain flour

8 tablespoons warm water,

6 teaspoons extra-virgin olive oil

4 pinches of salt

Serves 10

Brown the beef mince in olive oil and let it release any liquid, then fry gently on a mdium low heat for 15 minutes and leave to cool. You might want to use a blender on a low setting for the next step, otherwise just chop everything with a knife and mix it with you hands. Chop the mince, air-cured ham, and mortadella and mix well together. Squeeze all the milk out of the bread, chop it finely and stir it into the meat mixture. Add the eggs, parsley, Parmesan cheese, bread crumbs, thyme, black pepper, nutmeg and salt. Blend or mix everything together, until the filling is smooth and firm, with no lumps. This is important. Taste it, and adjust for salt, pepper and nutmeg.

PROCEDURE FOR THE PASTA

Make the pasta dough following the usual method, as explained in the previous chapter. Then make the tordelli following the procedure given in the previous recipes and cook them in abundant boiling salted water for about 8 minutes. Drain them and toss them in olive oil, place them in a large glass serving dish and cover them in Tuscan beef ragù (see page 232) with a sprinkling of grated Parmesan cheese on top. This is the traditional way to serve them in Lucca, dressed in ragù. This recipe is a classic in the Lucca area.

It's a slightly complex dish, because there is a lot of meat (both in the filling and the ragù on top) and we need to find a balance in the richness of the different meats. There are many different versions and variations in Lucca province, but this is my version which I have been preparing for years. You can also dress the tordelli in butter and sage, or tomato sauce or simply extra-virgin olive oil and thyme. Try it at home, preparing the tordelli with friends or family – usually when we make tordelli, we make a large quantity. Make it into an event, a collective synergy, a party or celebration.

Meat Main Courses

Braised Guinea-Fowl with Cutigliano Porcini Mushrooms

INGREDIENTS

1 guinea-fowl, around
   45 oz/1.3 kg
3 oz/80 g white onion
3 medium cloves garlic
3 sprigs rosemary, about
   6in/15cm long
10 sage leaves
2 bay leaves
7 tablespoons extra-virgin
   olive oil
7 fl oz/200ml dry white wine
3 oz/80 g dried porcini
   mushrooms from Cutigliano
5 oz/150 g organic tinned
   peeled tomatoes
vegetable stock no.3 (page 71)

Serves 5

Skin the guinea-fowl, apart from the wings and legs, and cut it into 2⅜in/6cm pieces. Wash them and dry them with a clean cloth. Soak the porcini mushrooms in warm water for at least 20 minutes, then rinse them carefully to remove any earth or impurities. Squeeze out as much water as possible and then chop them roughly and set them aside. You may come across recipes with dried porcini mushrooms that recommend you to filter the soaking water and then use it in the recipe. I don't do this, firstly because the mushroom water makes the dish harder to digest, and secondly because if the mushrooms are good quality they already have a strong taste, and the weak mushroom water doesn't really add anything to the final result.

Chop the onion, garlic cloves, rosemary and sage very finely, and fry in extra-virgin olive oil for a few minutes. Add the guinea-fowl and brown it on all sides. Pour over the white wine and cover everything with vegetable stock no.3, then cover the pan and simmer until the wine evaporates through the stock and there is no more smell of alcohol. Add the porcini mushrooms and stir. Crush the tinned tomatoes by hand, breaking them up into small pieces, add them to the pan and stir. Cover the pan and simmer for about 1 hour, then add salt, white pepper and nutmeg to taste. The guinea-fowl meat should be soft, but not falling off the bone. The dish should reflect the richness of the meat and mushrooms – tending towards brown, rather than red. The tomato should not overpower the other ingredients. Serve the guinea-fowl with a side dish of polenta or mashed potatoes or boiled potatoes. Cutigliano is a village in the mountains in the province of Pistoia, on the Tuscan-Emilian Apennine mountain range. It is well-known for the abundance of porcini mushrooms and chestnut trees in its forests.

Veal Ossobuco with White Onions and Black Peppercorns

INGREDIENTS

3 pieces of ossobuco or
   veal shanks, about
   14 oz/400 g each
35 oz/1 kg white onions
10 tablespoons extra-virgin
   olive oil
knob of butter
a handful of black peppercorns
5 fl oz/150 ml dry white wine
4 tablespoons 0 grade flour or
   plain flour
salt, vegetable stock no.4
   (page 71)

Serves 3

Lightly flour the veal shanks and brown them in a frying pan with 7 tablespoons of extra-virgin olive oil on a high heat. Take them out of the pan and wipe it clean with a piece of kitchen paper, then put it back on the heat with the remaining 3 tablespoons of extra-virgin olive oil and a knob of butter, on a medium heat. When the butter has melted put the veal shanks back in the pan and pour over the dry white wine and 2 ladlefuls of vegetable stock no.4. Cover the pan and continue to simmer. Slice the onions thinly and when the wine has evaporated through the stock (there is no more smell of alcohol), add them to the pan along with a handful of black peppercorns and a pinch of salt. Cover the pan and continue to simmer on a low heat for at least 1.5 hours until the veal is soft as butter. The onions will slowly melt into the sauce which will become creamy. Add a little more of the vegetable stock as needed if the sauce becomes too dry.

What can I say, ladies and gentlemen, boys and girls, men and women – if you want to win the heart of someone who likes veal, invite them for dinner and prepare this dish. It's a guaranteed success. It is delicate, the meat is soft, and the sauce is so delicious you'll need extra bread to mop it up. A simple but simply magnificent recipe.

Pork Loin in Beer and Breadcrumbs

INGREDIENTS

45 oz/1.3 kg pork loin

2 sprigs rosemary,
   6in/15cm long

8 large sage leaves

3 medium cloves garlic

10½ oz/300 g breadcrumbs

12 tablespoons extra-virgin
   olive oil

1¾ pint/1 litre pale craft beer
   or lager
(not double malt)

white pepper, nutmeg

salt, vegetable stock no.5
   (page 72)

butter

Serves 6

Preheat the oven to 200°C/400°F. Chop the rosemary, sage and garlic very finely, and mix in the white pepper and nutmeg. Press this mixture all over the pork loin, then roll it in the breadcrumbs and sprinkle it with salt. Line a roasting pan with baking paper and lay the meat in it. Drizzle the olive oil all over it and put it in the oven. When the meat has started to brown, take it out and turn it over. When it has browned on both sides, pour 25 fl oz/750 ml of the beer and 3 ladles of vegetable stock no.5 into the pan, and put it back in the oven to roast for 1.5 hours. Pierce the meat with a fork – if only a little clear liquid comes out, it is ready. Take the pork loin out of the pan and leave it to rest. Put the liquid from the pan into a small saucepan with the remaining 8 fl oz/250 ml of beer and a little vegetable stock, on a medium heat. Simmer this liquid until it has reduced to a gravy, then roll 2 knobs of butter in some plain flour and add to the saucepan. Stir well, taste, and add more white pepper and nutmeg if necessary. Slice the pork loin and arrange on a serving dish, pour the gravy on top and serve hot. The meat will be soft and the gravy should be creamy. As side dishes, I would recommend roast or mashed potatoes.

Braised Lamb in Chianti Wine

INGREDIENTS

45 oz/1.3 kg of lamb
(leg, shoulder or chops)

3½ oz/100 g onion

3 medium cloves garlic

4 sprigs rosemary, about
6in/15cm long

10 large sage leaves

2 bay leaves

7 tablespoons extra-virgin
olive oil

3 tablespoons 0 grade flour

1 bottle of Chianti wine,
25 fl oz/750 ml

7 oz/200 g organic tinned
peeled tomatoes

vegetable stock no.2 (page 70)

nutmeg, white pepper, salt

Serves 5

Cut the lamb into 2⅜in/6cm pieces. Rinse and pat dry with a clean cloth. Chop the onion, garlic, rosemary and sage very finely, and fry in extra-virgin olive oil for about 5 minutes, along with the bay leaves. Flour the pieces of lamb and brown them on all sides. Pour the whole bottle of Chianti wine into the pan, then add vegetable stock no.2 to cover everything. Cover the pan and simmer on a medium heat until the wine evaporates through the stock and there is no more smell of alcohol. Crush the tomatoes with your hands, breaking them up into small pieces, and add to the pan. Add salt, white pepper and nutmeg to taste. Continue cooking the lamb for about 1.5 hours, adding some more vegetable stock if the sauce dries up too much.

The finished dish should reflect the richness of the meat and the wine, a deep, intense reddish brown. I love this recipe because the taste of the meat is truly sublime. If there is any sauce left over after eating the meat, you can make tagliolini pasta the next day and use the sauce to dress them. Two recipes in one! This is very typical of the philosophy of Tuscan cuisine in particular, and cooking in general – don't waste anything. Use your imagination and love of cooking to create something new.

"Scottiglia" or Mixed Meat Stew, Arezzo Style

INGREDIENTS

88 oz/2.5 kg mixed meat
  and poultry
(guinea-fowl, chicken, pigeon,
duck, pork, veal)
3½ oz/100 g celery,
3½ oz/100 g onion
3½ oz/100 g carrot,
5 teaspoons chopped parsley
2 cloves, 8 juniper berries
10 tablespoons extra-virgin
  olive oil
10 fl oz/300 ml red wine
vegetable stock no.5 (page 72)
black pepper, salt

Serves 8

Prepare the meat by cutting it all into 2⅜in/6cm pieces, wash and pat dry with a clean cloth. Chop the celery, onion and carrot and fry in 10 tablespoons of extra-virgin olive oil for at least 5 minutes, along with the chopped parsley, cloves and juniper berries. Add the meat to the pan and brown it well on all sides. If the vegetables burn a little, that's fine. Pour over the red wine and enough vegetable stock no.5 to cover. Add a little salt and 7 twists of the pepper mill. Cover and simmer on a medium-low heat for about 2 hours, adding more vegetable stock as needed to prevent the sauce from drying up too much. In fact the Arezzo-style mixed meat stew should have a good quantity of sauce. Toast some homemade bread, rub it with a cut garlic clove and serve the meat stew in an earthenware or terracotta dish with the garlic bread on the side.

There are lots of possible variations on this recipe, because of the types of meat used. Farmers used whatever they had available, so the meat can vary according to the season. It's a rich dish, strong on the palate. Pair it with a full-bodied red wine, I would suggest a Brunello di Montalcino or Montepulciano.

"Peposo" or Tuscan Peppery Beef Stew

INGREDIENTS

53 oz/1.5 kg stewing beef
10 cloves unpeeled garlic
2 generous handfuls black
    peppercorns
2 oz/50 g tomato purèe
1¾ pint/1 litre red wine

Serves 5

Cut the beef into 1¼in/3cm chunks. Put it in a large saucepan with the garlic cloves, peppercorns, concentrated tomato purèe and the wine. Cover and cook on a very low heat, simmering very gently for about 3 hours. You don't need stock, nor oil, nor salt. When cooked to perfection, the beef should be as soft as butter. This slow-cooking technique really brings out the delicious taste of the meat and the black pepper. If the sauce is a bit liquid when the meat is cooked, roll a knob of butter in some plain flour and stir it into the peposo to make it creamy. Serve piping hot in earthenware bowls with slices of garlic-rubbed toasted homemade bread on the side, and wash it all down with an excellent Chianti wine.

Those who love this historic dish take it very seriously. It was developed by the Florentine furnace-workers or 'fornacini' who baked the terracotta tiles for the dome on the cathedral of Santa Maria in Fiore in the centre of Florence. It is also known as Peposo del Brunelleschi, named for the architect of the cathedral. Of course, at the time tomatoes had not yet arrived in Europe so the original recipe certainly did not contain tomato purèe. The labourers would put a pan of meat and wine and peppercorns just inside the hot furnace, where it cooked slowly for 5 or 6 hours. The peppercorns were probably to disguise the strong taste of meat that was less than fresh – we are talking about the Renaissance era, a time in which food preservation was very difficult. It's a historic and important recipe, born from the vitality and creativity of the Renaissance period.

Fish Main Courses

Shrimps in Brandy and Tomato Sauce

INGREDIENTS

25 large king shrimps
   (prawns), fresh
   or top quality frozen
2 large cloves garlic
2 teaspoons chopped parsley
2 small dried chilli peppers
10 tablespoons extra-virgin
   olive oil
1 espresso cup excellent brandy
14 oz/400 g organic puréed
   tomatoes
shellfish stock no.7 (page 73)
white pepper, salt

Serves 5

Chop the garlic and chilli pepper very finely and mix with the chopped parsley. Fry this mixture in olive oil in a large frying pan for about 2 minutes, then add the whole shrimps and cook for about 3 minutes. Pour over the brandy, if possible flambé the shrimps (use a lighter) then cook for a further 5 minutes and pour in the tomatoes. Use the best quality you can find, as the lower acidity is very important for this recipe to work well. Add a little salt and pepper. Cook for another 10 minutes on a medium heat, and if the sauce becomes too dry add some concentrated shellfish stock no.7.

This recipe can also be done without the tomatoes – just use the stock alone. Serve 5 shrimps on each plate, with the sauce. Correct table etiquette probably forbids it, but there is nothing like slowly peeling these shrimps and getting sauce all over your hands. Your guests will be licking their fingers, and cleaning their plates with bread. These might be vulgar gestures to some, but to a chef it's the greatest compliment. Thank you!

Sea Bream and Wild Fennel al Cartoccio

INGREDIENTS

1 fillet sea bream about
  20 oz/600 g

3 fresh tomato slices about
  ½in/1cm thick

3 small cloves garlic

2 sprigs wild fennel fronds

5 tablespoons extra-virgin
  olive oil

5 fl oz/150 ml dry white wine

black pepper

salt

Serves 2

Preheat the oven to 200°C/400°F. Take a sheet of foil and form it into a kind of boat shape by scrunching up the ends. Grease the inside with olive oil and lay the fish fillet on it. Lay the tomato slices beside the fish, along with the unpeeled garlic and the fennel fronds. Sprinkle salt and pepper, pour over the white wine and cover with another piece of foil. Put the foil parcel in a baking tray, pour water into the tray to a depth of ¾in/2cm, and bake for 15 to 20 minutes, depending on the thickness of the fillet. After 15 minutes check the fish – if it is soft but white all the way through, it is ready. Serve hot with roast vegetables or Florentine peas or green beans with hazelnuts, almonds and redcurrants (see Chapter on Side Dishes). This recipe is quick, simple and delicious. If you can't find wild fennel, try 3 sprigs of fresh marjoram.

Gurnard Fish, Livorno Style

INGREDIENTS

5 gurnard about
   9 oz/250 g each
5 medium garlic cloves
3 small dried chilli peppers
3 tablespoons chopped parsley
8 tablespoons extra-virgin
   olive oil
17½ oz/500 g organic
   tinned peeled tomatoes
3¼ fl oz/100 ml dry
   white wine
black pepper, salt

Serves 5

Chop the garlic and chilli peppers very finely, mix with the chopped parsley and fry this mixture in olive oil for about 2 minutes. Break the tomatoes up with your hands or very briefly use a handheld blender, then add them to the pan with a pinch of sugar to counter the acidity of the tomato. Simmer for at least 20 minutes. Put the fish in the pan and pour over the white wine, cover and continue simmering on a medium heat for 10 minutes. Add a little salt to taste.

Gurnard is a very popular fish in Tuscany, it can be used for fish stews and pasta dishes, and also as a main course as in this recipe or baked in the oven. Its flesh is very tasty and contains many minerals such as potassium, calcium, phosphorous and magnesium, plus vitamins A and D. It also contains very little fat. It's not expensive and tastes good. Accompany this dish with a green salad and a good Vermentino white wine.

Octopus "In Galera"
with Potatoes and Parsley

INGREDIENTS

53 oz/1.5 kg baby octopus

2 large cloves garlic

5 tablespoons chopped parsley

3 oz/80 g pine nuts

8 tablespoons extra-virgin
   olive oil

7 fl oz/200ml dry white wine

1 lemon

35 oz/1 kg floury potatoes

vegetable stock no.2 (page 70)

black pepper

salt

Serves 5

Clean the octopus, removing beaks and innards, leave the skin on if the octopus are small. Rinse them and dry them with a cloth, then cut into chunks. Chop the garlic and pine nuts very finely and mix with 3 tablespoons of the chopped parsley. Fry this mixture in olive oil for about 4 minutes. Add the octopus, fry for 5 minutes, then pour over the wine. Cover and cook for at least 30 minutes. If it dries up too much, add some vegetable stock no.2. Cut the potatoes into 1¼in/3cm chunks and add to the pan, along with salt and pepper to taste. Cover and cook for another 20 minutes, then squeeze the lemon over the octopus and sprinkle over 2 tablespoons of chopped parsley. Take the pan off the heat and leave the finished dish to rest for a few minutes before serving. If the octopus is good and fresh, this dish is divinely reminiscent of the sea. It reminds me how, as a boy, my cousin and I would go fishing with our nets in a little boat, and we would dive straight into the water to catch any octopus which escaped from the net. The name 'in galera' means 'in prison', and probably refers to the long cooking time during which the octopus is imprisoned in the covered pan.

Squid and Chard in Tomato "Zimino"

INGREDIENTS

70 oz/2 kg small to medium
    sized squid

3 medium cloves garlic

2 small chilli peppers

1 sprig rosemary about
    6in/15cm long

8 tablespoons extra-virgin
    olive oil

7 fl oz/200ml dry white wine

20 oz/600 g chard leaves

9 oz/250 g organic tinned
    peeled tomatoes

white pepper

salt, fish stock no.6 (page 73)

Serves 5

Clean your squid, rinse and cut into 1½in/4cm pieces. Pull the rosemary needles from the stalk and chop them very finely along with the garlic and chilli peppers. Fry this mixture in olive oil for about 2 minutes and then add the squid pieces. After about 5 minutes pour over the white wine, allow it to evaporate a little and then cover everything with fish stock no.6. Simmer for about 10 minutes. When the wine has evaporated (there is no more smell of alcohol), add the chard leaves and the tinned tomatoes, broken up into pieces by hand. Add a little salt and white pepper. Cover the pan and cook on a medium high heat for at least 1 hour, until the squid become soft as butter. Add more fish stock as necessary if the sauce becomes too dry.

This squid stew already contains vegetables, so serve it with a side dish of good quality polenta, or on top of toasted garlic-rubbed bread. This recipe is much loved in Tuscany. I remember when I worked in Lucca in a famous restaurant in the historic town centre, people would phone the restaurant to order this dish. As fast as we could make it, they ate it. It was wonderful to see people so enthusiastic as they ate. What a pleasure!

Salt Cod with Cherry Tomatoes, Raisins and Nuts

INGREDIENTS

1 fillet of salt cod, about
   35 oz/1 kg, already
   soaked and ready to be
   cooked
4 tablespoons 0 grade or
   plain flour
20 oz/600 g fresh cherry
   tomatoes
3½ oz/100 g raisins
10½ oz/300 g mixture of
   pine nuts, hazelnuts,
   almonds, pumpkin seeds,
   dried redcurrants)
3 medium garlic cloves
8 tablespoons extra-virgin
   olive oil
5 fl oz/150 ml dry white wine
4 teaspoons chopped parsley
white pepper
vegetable stock no.5 (page 72)
salt

Serves 3

Cut the salt cod fillet into 3 pieces. Peel the garlic cloves, cut them in half and fry them in a large non-stick pan in olive oil for 2 minutes. Quarter the cherry tomatoes and mix them in a bowl with the nuts, pumpkin seeds, redcurrants and raisins. Add this to the garlic in the pan and fry for 2 minutes on a high heat, then add the fish and pour over the white wine. Cover and cook for 20 minutes, shaking the pan every now and again to make sure nothing is sticking. You can add some vegetable stock if necessary. Check for salt and add some if needed but the cod is already quite salty. Sprinkle with the chopped parsley and serve.

This recipe is quite original and interesting for combination of the sweetness of the raisins and redcurrants with the crunchiness of the nuts.

Sea Bass All'isolana

INGREDIENTS

3 sea bass, approximately
   14 oz/400 g each

5 cloves garlic

6 sprigs rosemary
   4in/10cm long

3 vine tomatoes

53 oz/1.5 kg floury potatoes

7 fl oz/200ml dry white wine

1¾ pint/1 litre sunflower oil
   for frying potatoes

9 tablespoons extra-virgin
   olive oil

white pepper

salt

Serves 6

Prehat the oven to 220°C/425°F. Gut and scale the fish. Rinse inside and out, then dry them and put a garlic clove, a sprig of rosemary, a pinch of salt and pepper inside each fish. Slice the potatoes ½in/1cm thick and fry in plenty of sunflower oil. When they start to turn light brown around the edges, they are ready. Put them on some kitchen paper to absorb any excess oil. The potatoes will be tastier and softer because they have been pre-fried. If we used them raw for this recipe, they would not cook fully. Slice the tomatoes ½in/1cm thick. Line a baking pan with baking paper and grease it with extra-virgin olive oil. Lay the potatoes out in one layer. Sprinkle with a little salt, then make a layer with the tomato slices and a little salt again. Lay the fish on top of the tomatoes, drizzle with 9 tablespoons of olive oil and then pour over the wine. Sprinkle with white pepper and bake for 20 minutes. Check whether they are cooked by making an incision along the side. To serve the fish, remove the heads and skin, which should come away easily, then use a knife to remove the fillets from both sides of the spine. Serve each fish with 3 or 4 slices of potato and a few slices of tomato, a drizzle of olive oil and a sprinkling of white pepper.

This recipe is very popular in restaurants along the Versilia coast and in the province of Lucca. It's convenient because you cook the fish along with its side dish of potatoes and tomatoes, and it's also elegant and delicate, seductive almost.

SALE LA STRADA BIANCA
TRA I MELI SELVATICI E LE VITI
SINO ALL'ULTIMO POGGIO:
IL BORGO SEVERO FRA I CIPRESSI
CORONA LA COLLINA
CHE SI VESTE D'ULIVI E DI GINESTRE.
MI SENTO PARTE ANCH'IO
DELL'OPERAR DEGLI ABITANTI ANTICHI
DI QUESTA DOLCE TERRA
E QUI VORREI FINIR L'OPERA MIA
MONTEBENICHI.

Side Dishes

Mixed Roast Vegetables

INGREDIENTS

3½ oz/100 g yellow pepper

7 oz/200 g carrot

7 oz/200 g onion

5 oz/150 g pale zucchini
(courgettes)

5 oz/150 g celery

7 oz/200 g potatoes

9 tablespoons extra-virgin
olive oil

white pepper

salt

Serves 5

Wash the vegetables and cut them into 1 ¼in/3cm chunks. Line a baking tray with baking paper, spread the vegetables on it and drizzle them with 9 tablespoons of extra-virgin olive oil. Mix the vegetables with your hands so they are evenly coated with the oil. Bake at 200°C/400°F for about 20 minutes. Take the tray out of the oven and sprinkle with white pepper and 5 pinches of salt. Mix again with your hands. Put the tray back in the oven for another 10 minutes and your vegetables are ready. The salt needs to be added after the vegetables have been part-roasted because otherwise they become soft and limp instead of remaining solid and shiny with a good texture. This is a simple recipe, but very attractive to the eyes and palate. I don't add any herbs to this recipe because I prefer to preserve the real taste of the vegetables – each one different to the others, but together creating a wonderful synergy of the ingredients. This is a perfect accompaniment to braised white meat dishes, legume salads and all the main fish dishes in this book.

Flask-Cooked Borlotti Beans with Bay Leaves

INGREDIENTS

9 oz/250 g dried organic
   borlotti beans

5 medium garlic cloves,
   unpeeled

5 bay leaves

30 black peppercorns

3 tablespoons extra-virgin
   olive oil

½ tablespoon coarse sea salt

Serves 5

Soak the beans in cold water for at least 12 hours or overnight. Rinse them and put them in your glass flask or an earthenware crock pot with 2½ pints/2 litres of cold water, along with the unpeeled garlic cloves, bay leaves, peppercorns, extra-virgin olive oil and the coarse sea salt. Use a gas stove flame spreader under the flask and bring to the boil, then turn down the heat and simmer for about 40 minutes. Taste the beans – they are ready when they are soft and creamy inside but the skins remain whole and are not falling apart. Serve hot with a drizzle of extra-virgin olive oil and a generous sprinkling of black pepper. The bay leaves give a strong taste to this very distinctive recipe, which is a good accompaniment for salt cod dishes or meats braised in wine.

Classic Flask-Cooked Cannellini Beans

INGREDIENTS

17½ oz/500 g dried organic
   cannellini beans

8 garlic cloves, unpeeled

25 whole sage leaves

40 black peppercorns

4 tablespoons extra-virgin
   olive oil

1 tbsp coarse sea salt

Serves 5

Soak the beans in cold water for at least 12 hours or overnight. Put the beans in your glass flask or an earthenware crock pot with 6¼ pints/3 litres of cold water, along with the unpeeled garlic cloves, sage leaves, peppercorns, extra-virgin olive oil and the coarse sea salt. Use a gas stove flame spreader under the flask and bring to the boil, then turn down the heat and simmer for about 40 minutes. Taste the beans – they are ready when they are soft and creamy inside but the skins remain whole and are not falling apart.

Flask-cooked beans or "fagioli al fiasco" is a very old recipe using a cooking method that was perfect for the long winter days in the Tuscan countryside. The beans would be slowly cooked in an old Chianti wine flask beside the fireplace, and this long cooking time gave them an extraordinary softness and intense taste. Serve the beans hot, and I suggest that you try them with lamb cooked in Chianti wine or veal ossobuco with onions. The half kilo quantity of dried beans used in this recipe is quite abundant, which means that once cooked, half of them can be made into "cannellini all'uccelletto", which is the next recipe.

Cannellini Beans All'uccelletto

INGREDIENTS

9 oz/250 g flask-cooked
    cannellini beans
4 medium cloves garlic
20 medium fresh sage leaves
12½ oz/350 g organic
    tinned peeled tomatoes
6 tablespoons extra-virgin
    olive oil
white pepper
salt, brown sugar

Serves 5

Use half the cannellini beans that you cooked in a flask the day before. Drain them and keep a little of the cooking water. Pick out and throw away the cooked garlic, sage and some of the peppercorns. Cut the 4 new garlic cloves in half, and fry with the fresh sage leaves in the extra-virgin olive oil for about 3 minutes. Blend the tomatoes very briefly – they mustn't lose their redness, which will happen if you blend them for too long, and they should be roughly chopped, not purèed. Add the tomatoes to the garlic and sage and simmer for about 20 minutes. Then add the beans with a little of the cooking water. Stir in 4 pinches of salt and a pinch of brown sugar, 6 twists of white pepper from the pepper mill, and the job is done. Your beans will have a very creamy sauce and an explosive delicious taste.

Florentine Peas

INGREDIENTS

28 oz/800 g fresh peas (or
   frozen organic top quality)

5 oz/150 g thin sliced pancetta

7 oz/200 g white onion

8 tablespoons extra-virgin
   olive oil

vegetable stock no.1 (page 70)

black pepper

salt

Serves 5

Finely chop the onion, cut the pancetta into ¾in/2cm pieces, and fry together in 8 tablespoons of extra-virgin olive oil for about 5 minutes. Add the peas and cook for a further 20 minutes at least on a high heat, adding vegetable stock no.1 as needed. Stir in 5 pinches of salt and a sprinkling of black pepper and the Florentine peas are ready. I find the onion brings out the sweetness of the peas, and if you use fresh peas in the spring season they are exceptionally good. This is an excellent accompaniment for all white meat dishes.

Green Beans in Tomato

INGREDIENTS

25 oz/700 g green beans

5 oz/150 g onion

4 cloves garlic

8 tablespoons extra-virgin
  olive oil

14 oz/400 g organic tinned
  peeled tomatoes

vegetable stock no.3 (page 71)

black pepper

salt

Serves 5

Wash the beans, top and tail them and boil in lightly salted water for about 10 minutes. Drain in a colander. Chop the onion very finely, cut the garlic cloves in half and fry together in extra-virgin olive oil for about 3 minutes. Squeeze the tomatoes into pieces with your hands, add them to the pan and cook for 5 minutes. Add the beans, 4 pinches of salt and 4 twists of the pepper mill and stir well. Cook for another 15 minutes on a medium heat, adding a little vegetable stock no. 3.

Help yourself with the vegetable broth 3 which I call 'enriched' because it's nutritious, tasty and light. These beans go well with any main meat course, or simple main fish course. The fresher the beans, the better this dish is.

Green Beans with Nuts and Redcurrants

INGREDIENTS

25 oz/700 g green beans

5 oz/150 g finely chopped
  onion

1 oz/30 g pumpkin seeds,

1½ oz/40 g almonds
  (unpeeled)

1½ oz/40 g hazelnuts (peeled)

1½ oz/40 g organic dried
  redcurrants (if you can't find
  them, you can use organic
  raisins)

6 tablespoons extra-virgin
  olive oil

vegetable stock no.1
  (page 70)

white pepper, salt

Serves 5

Wash the beans and trim the ends. Boil them in salted water for about 15 minutes. Meanwhile, chop the onion quite finely and fry it with 6 tablespoons of extra-virgin olive oil for at least 7 minutes on a medium-low heat. Then add the pumpkin seeds, almonds, hazelnuts and redcurrants. Fry for another 4 minutes, then add the beans along with 4 pinches of salt and 4 of pepper, and mix well to amalgamate all the ingredients. Continue cooking for 5 minutes, adding a little vegetable stock no.1 as needed. This side dish is an interesting combination and works well with main meat dishes that don't contain tomato, or any fish dish.

Sweet and Sour Borettane Onions

INGREDIENTS

28 oz/800 g Borrettane onions

5 tablespoons extra-virgin
   olive oil

4 tablespoons organic
   brown sugar

8 tablespoons white wine
   vinegar

3 pinches of salt

vegetable stock no.1 (page 70)

Serves 5

Peel, wash and dry the onions and remove any remaining roots. Fry them on a high heat with the extra-virgin olive oil for 5 minutes. Add the brown sugar and cook for another 5 minutes to caramelise it. Add the white wine vinegar and the salt. Cover and continue cooking for another 10 minutes, adding a little vegetable stock no.1 as necessary, and a few drops of vinegar if needed. When the onions are cooked on the outside but still slightly crunchy in the centre and the sweet and sour is well balanced, the onions are ready.

You can follow the same procedure using a top quality balsamic vinegar instead of white wine vinegar, or use balsamic vinegar as a garnish on the plate. These onions are an excellent side dish for fish dishes such as sea bream in cartoccio and sea bass all'isolana. For meat, I would recommend pork shin with apples and pork loin in beer.

Braised String Beans
with Garlic and Pepper

INGREDIENTS

28 oz/800 g green Tuscan
  string beans

5 medium cloves garlic

4 small dried chilli peppers

8 tablespoons extra-virgin
  olive oil

17½ oz/500 g organic
  tinned peeled tomatoes

salt, vegetable stock no.3
  (page 71)

Serves 5

Tuscan string beans are very long, very thin green beans, which we serve whole. In Italian they are called 'stringhe'. Wash the beans and trim the ends. Boil them in salted water for at least 10 minutes, then drain them. Cut the garlic cloves and chilli peppers in half and fry them in olive oil for about 2 minutes on a medium-low heat. Chop the tomatoes by hand and add them to the pan, along with the beans. Add 4 pinches of salt and cover the beans with vegetable stock no.3. Simmer on a low heat until the stock has reduced and the tomato is quite dry. The beans should be al dente when you add them to the tomatoes, so they acquire more taste as they finish cooking in the tomato sauce. Personally, I could eat an entire frying pan of these sweet green beans. They are one of the vegetable recipes that I am literally crazy about. This is a good accompaniment for all tomato-based main courses, both meat and fish.

Val D'arno Peperonata, My Style

INGREDIENTS

14 oz/400 g yellow pepper

14 oz/400 g red pepper

2 large cloves garlic,

5 oz/150 g onion

20 salted capers (rinse in
   fresh water)

3 oz/80 g pine nuts

4 tablespoons finely chopped
   parsley

2 oz/50 g finely chopped
   red pepper

7 tablespoons extra-virgin
   olive oil

white pepper, salt, vegetable
   stock no.4 (page 71)

Serves 5

When you prepare the vegetable stock no.4, use very little salt as the capers in this recipe are already very salty. Wash the red and yellow peppers, remove the stalks and seeds inside, then chop them into 2in/5cm pieces. Rinse the salted capers. Chop the garlic, onion, capers and pine nuts very finely. Mix them with the finely chopped red pepper and parsley, and fry this mixture in olive oil for at least 4 minutes. Add the rest of the pepper pieces and cook on a high heat for another 5 minutes, adding the vegetable stock as needed. Add white pepper to taste.

The original recipe also contains potatoes, zucchinis (courgettes) and tomatoes. I modified it using a traditional peperonata as inspiration, which then evolved into a different but splendid combination, born from practical experience in my kitchen.

Cauliflower "Strascicato"

INGREDIENTS

1 cauliflower approximately
   35 oz/1 kg

½ lemon

4 medium cloves garlic

2 small dried chilli peppers

30 Tuscan black olives (or
   Kalamata)

7 tablespoons extra-virgin olive
   oil

17½ oz/500 g organic
   tinned peeled tomatoes

black pepper

salt, vegetable stock no.1
   (page 70)

Serves 5

Wash the cauliflower, cut it into quarters, and cook it in salted water with half a lemon for about 10 minutes. Drain it and leave to cool. Cut the garlic cloves and chilli peppers in half, and fry them in olive oil for 2 minutes. Squeeze the tomatoes into pieces with your hands, add them to the pan and cook for a further 10 minutes on a medium heat. Cut the cauliflower into 1½in/4cm pieces and add to the pan. Slice the olive flesh from the stones and mix in with the cauliflower. Carry on cooking for another 15 minutes, adding a little vegetable stock no.1 as necessary to prevent the cauliflower from sticking. Add black pepper, but only a little salt as the black olives are already very salty.

Cauliflower is always very good, but as a side dish it is underrated by most restaurants in Italy. It's actually a very good accompaniment, and balances the meal. The term 'strascicato' refers to the way the cauliflower is dragged or wiped round the pan as it cooks, so it absorbs all the tomato and stock.

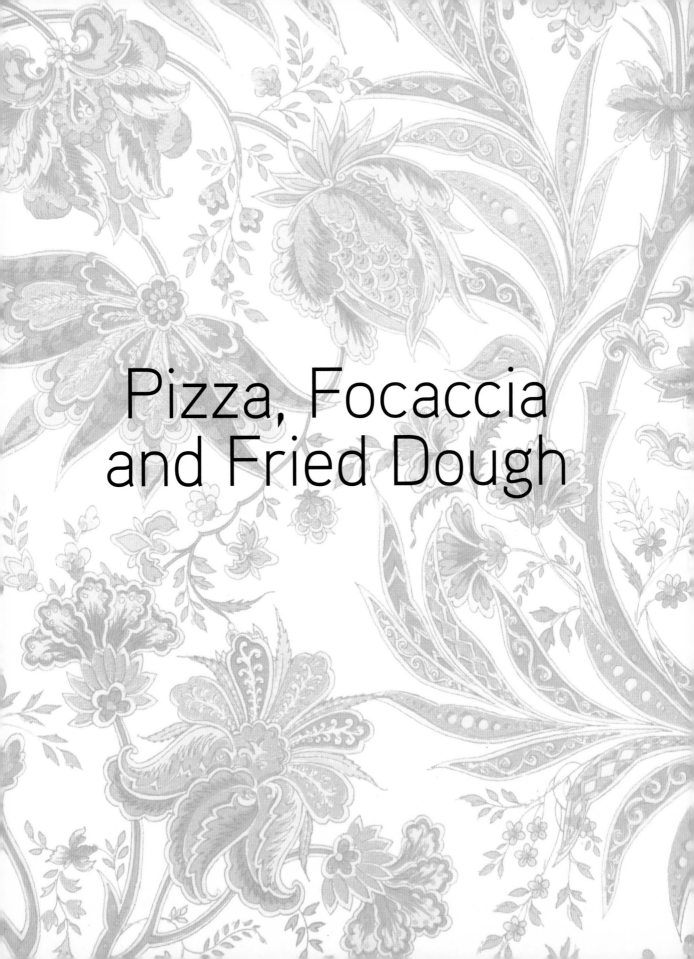

Pizza, Focaccia and Fried Dough

My Rustic Pizza

INGREDIENTS FOR THE DOUGH FOR 2 PIZZAS

10 fl oz/300 ml warm water

4 pinches salt

5 tablespoons rice milk

2 tablespoons extra-virgin olive oil

½ oz/12 g fresh yeast

23–25 oz/650–700g 0 grade flour or plain flour

Serves 4

Preheat the oven to 200°C/400°F. Put the warm water, salt, rice milk, extra-virgin olive oil and yeast in a large glass bowl. Stir well with a fork until the yeast dissolves. Sieve in the flour and mix well until you form a soft, smooth dough, not too sticky. Start with 23 oz/650 g of flour and add the extra 2 oz/50 g little by little if needed, as you knead the dough. Cover and leave the dough to rise in a warm place for an hour and a half. Knead again and divide it in half. Put each half in a separate bowl, cover and leave to rise again for at least another hour and a half. Line a 13¾in/35cm circular baking pan with baking paper and grease lightly with olive oil. Put one of the dough balls in the middle of the pan, and press it out with your hands (greased lightly with olive oil to prevent the dough sticking to them) until it covers the base of the pan. Spread the tomato sauce on top, and bake for about 6 minutes. Take the pizza out of the oven, add the toppings according to your recipe, then put it back in the oven for another 10 minutes. These cooking times are referred to a domestic oven, obviously if you have the chance to use a professional oven the cooking times will be significantly reduced.

Pizza NO.1

INGREDIENTS

2 small pale zucchinis
  (courgettes)

½ yellow pepper, cut into strips

15 Tuscan olives in brine (or
  Kalamata olives)

15 fresh asparagus tips

10 cherry tomatoes

5 oz/150 g organic
  tomato puree

3 pinches dried oregano

1 pinch organic brown sugar

3 pinches of salt

3 tablespoons extra-virgin
  olive oil

1 clove garlic

10 basil leaves

7 oz/200 g fresh mozzarella

Prepare the tomato sauce for the pizza. Put the tomato purée in a bowl and add the oregano, sugar, salt, olive oil, clove of garlic cut in half and basil leaves torn in half. Stir until the salt and sugar dissolve and the sauce is ready to be used. Cut the zucchinis into ½in/1cm cubes, cut the pepper into thin strips and cut the tomatoes in half. Chop the mozzarella into tiny cubes. After cooking the tomato-topped pizza for the initial 6 minutes, add the toppings, a drizzle of extra-virgin olive oil and a sprinkling of salt, and finish cooking it. This is a delicious combination of toppings, I like vegetarian pizzas very much for their delicious and wonderful fragrance.

Pizza NO.2

INGREDIENTS

20 pieces artichokes in oil

5 slices eggplant (aubergine)

7 slices zucchini (courgette)

15 Tuscan olives in brine (or
Kalamata olives)

5 oz/150 g organic
tomato puree

3 pinches dried thyme

1 pinch organic brown sugar

3 pinches of salt

3 tablespoons extra-virgin
olive oil

1 clove garlic

10 basil leaves

White pepper

7 oz/200 g fresh mozzarella

Chop the basil leaves finely with a knife. Prepare the tomato sauce for the pizza. Put the tomato purèe in a bowl and add the dried thyme, sugar, salt, extra-virgin olive oil, clove of garlic cut in half, chopped basil and white pepper. Mix well with a fork until the sugar and salt dissolve. Let the sauce rest for a while to develop the taste of the ingredients. Drain the artichokes from their oil, and grill the eggplant and zucchinis. Chop the mozzarella into tiny cubes. After cooking the tomato-topped pizza for the initial 6 minutes, add the toppings, a drizzle of extra-virgin olive oil, a sprinkling of salt and another 2 pinches of thyme and finish cooking it. This pizza is both nutritious and delicious.

Pizza NO.3

INGREDIENTS

14 oz/400 g Tuscan kale or
  black cabbage
(2 cloves garlic, 4 tablespoons
  olive oil, 2 dried chilli
  peppers and salt for cooking
  the cabbage)
12 cherry tomatoes
15 Tuscan olives in brine or
  Kalamata olives
20 salted capers
5 oz/150 g organic tomato
  puree
1 large pinch each of dried
  marjoram, dried thyme and
  dried oregano
1 pinch organic brown sugar
3 pinches of salt
1 clove garlic
10 basil leaves
Grated black pepper
7 oz/200 g fresh mozzarella

Wash the kale, cut off the hard stems and boil the leaves in salted water for about 5 minutes. Drain and squeeze out the excess water. Fry the kale in a pan for about 8 minutes with the garlic, olive oil, chopped chilli peppers and a pinch of salt and set it aside. Prepare the tomato sauce for the pizza. Put the tomato purèe in a bowl and add the dried herbs, sugar, salt and black pepper, clove of garlic cut in half, and basil leaves torn in half. Stir until the salt and sugar dissolve. Chop the mozzarella into tiny cubes. After cooking the tomato-topped pizza for the initial 6 minutes, add the toppings and a drizzle of extra-virgin olive oil, and finish cooking it. Top it with the hot cooked kale and serve immediately. This is my favourite pizza for the winter – the addition of the cooked kale really enriches the taste and it's an interesting combination.

Mixed Seed Wholemeal Focaccia

INGREDIENTS

16 fl oz/500 ml warm water

5 pinches of salt

2 tablespoons extra-virgin
   olive oil

½ oz/12 g fresh yeast

30 oz/850 g flour (half
   wholemeal, half white)

7 oz/200 g organic mixed
   seeds (sesame, sunflower
   and poppy)

Serves 5

Preheat the oven to 200°C/400°F, fan-assisted if possible. Put the water, salt, extra-virgin olive oil and yeast into a large bowl and mix well with a fork until the yeast has dissolved. Stir in the flour and mix until you have a smooth, soft dough. Cover it and leave it in a warm place to rise for about 3 hours, kneading it again at the end of every hour. Line your baking pan with baking paper and grease it lightly with olive oil. Add the seeds and knead them into the dough until they are evenly distributed, then put the dough in the pan and flatten it with your hands, pressing it well into the corners. Sprinkle with a few more mixed seeds and bake for about 15 minutes. Like all food, this focaccia should be thoroughly chewed to fully appreciate the mixed seeds, which have wonderful nutritional properties in general. Sesame seeds in particular have a high content of iron, calcium, phosphorous and magnesium which strengthen and support the immune system. Sunflower seeds are rich in vitamins that combat cellular ageing and are essential to the metabolic pathways in the body. Poppy seeds favour the uptake of protein, contain a lot of fatty acid Omega-6 and vitamin E, and help control blood sugar levels. This is a superb focaccia from every point of view.

Mixed Wholemeal Focaccia

INGREDIENTS

13½ fl oz/400 ml warm water

½ oz/10 g fresh yeast

2 tablespoons extra-virgin
   olive oil

3 large pinches of salt

17½–20 oz/500–600g
   organic wholemeal flour
(wheat, rye and spelt mix if
   possible)

Serves 5

Preheat the oven to 200°C/400°F. Put the water, yeast, extra-virgin olive oil and salt in a large bowl and stir with a fork until the yeast dissolves completely. Add the flour and mix until you have a smooth, soft dough. The exact amount of flour needed varies according to the type of flour used, and also whether it has been stone-ground or not, and bear in mind that wholemeal flours have a higher humidity level than white flours, so working with them is a little different. Start with 17½ oz/500 g and add the extra 3½ oz/100 g little by little as needed. Knead the dough, cover it and leave it in a warm, dry place to rise for 3 hours. Knead it at the end of every hour and leave it to rise again. Line a 13¾in/35cm diameter baking pan with baking paper, lightly grease the paper and your hands with extra-virgin olive oil. Put the dough in the middle of the pan and press it out to the edges with your hands. Sprinkle with salt and bake for about 15 minutes. The focaccia should be crispy on the outside, fragrant and soft on the inside. When we eat in general, but particularly when we eat wholemeal foods like this one (which should always be made with organic flour), we should chew every mouthful slowly and thoroughly to assist the digestive process in the body. Wholemeal flour nourishes the body and revitalises it. This focaccia will take you back in time, it is rustic and evocative.

Simple Tuscan Focaccia with Oregano

INGREDIENTS

16 fl oz/500 ml warm
   water
4 pinches of salt
1 tablespoon extra-virgin
   olive oil
½ oz/10 g fresh yeast
23 oz/650 g 0 grade
   flour or plain flour
dried origano

Serves 5

Preheat the oven to 200°C/400°F. Put the water, yeast, salt and extra-virgin olive oil into a large bowl, and mix well with a fork until the yeast has dissolved. Add the flour and continue to mix until you form a smooth, soft and sticky dough. Cover the dough and put it in a dry warm place to rise for 3 hours. At the end of each hour, press it down with a fork and leave it to rise again. Line a 13¾in/35cm circular baking pan or tray with baking paper and grease it lightly with 3 tablespoons of extra-virgin olive oil. Put the dough in the centre of the pan, grease your hands with olive oil to prevent the dough from sticking to them and press it out to cover the tray, being careful to press it out well to the edge of the pan. Drizzle over another 3 tablespoons of extra-virgin olive oil, sprinkle with 4 pinches of salt and as much dried oregano as you like, and bake for about 15 minutes. The focaccia should be crisp and crunchy on the outside, soft and fragrant on the inside. It is delicious as it is, or sliced and filled with ham and pecorino cheese. In addition to the oregano, you could also top it with sliced vine tomatoes before putting it in the oven. You can make two types of focaccia in one, by pressing halved cherry tomatoes and sage leaves into one half and putting thinly sliced red onion and rosemary needles into the other half. Sprinkle with salt and freshly ground black pepper. For all these little variations, the cooking time remains the same.

In my house we make fresh focaccia every day, and it often replaces the bread on our table. My son loves it, and always helps me to prepare it. 'Bona' as we say in Tuscany – very good!

Simple Fried Dough Balls

INGREDIENTS

16 fl oz/500 ml warm water

4 pinches of salt

3 tablespoons extra-virgin
   olive oil

½ oz/12 g fresh yeast

30 oz/850 g 0 grade flour
   or plain flour

1¾ pint/1 litre sunflower oil

Serves 8

Put the water, salt, extra-virgin olive oil and yeast into a large bowl. Mix well with a fork until the yeast dissolves completely. Add the flour and stir until you have a soft and sticky dough. Cover it and leave to rise in a warm dry place for 3 hours. At the end of every hour, press the dough down with a fork and leave it to rise again. Heat the sunflower oil in a saucepan on a medium high heat. To check when the oil is hot enough for frying, drop in a small pinch of flour – if it sizzles and fries immediately, the oil is ready. Using two tablespoons, drop spoonfuls of dough into the hot oil and fry them for 3 minutes. Drain the dough balls on kitchen paper, sprinkle them with salt and serve immediately.

This is one recipe amongst many for the fried dough balls that are commonly eaten in every region in Italy, but they are widely used in Tuscany as an appetiser, accompanied by salami and pecorino cheese, or simply used to substitute bread on the table. In Tuscany, fried dough balls have many names, according to the area and local custom. You may see them being called panzanella, cencini, coccole, pupporine (from the word 'puppora' which means small breasts), panzerotti, focaccini fritti etc. They are quite delicious and everyone likes them. You can serve them as finger food in a buffet. You can slice them open and fill them with cured ham or cooked ham, pecorino cheese, soft cheese or a mixture of any of these, or try filling them with vegetables. They are extremely tempting, and I imagine by now you simply can't wait to try them. Enjoy!

Fried Herby Dough Balls

INGREDIENTS

20 fl oz/600 ml warm water

5 pinches of salt

4 tablespoons extra-virgin
  olive oil

¾ oz/15 g fresh yeast

33 oz/950 g 0 grade flour
  or plain flour

3 sprigs of rosemary about
  6in/15cm long

15 medium sage leaves

4 pinches dried oregano

4 pinches dried thyme

Black pepper

1¾ pint/1 litre sunflower oil

Serves 8

Put the water, salt, extra-virgin olive oil and yeast into a large bowl. Stir with a fork until the yeast has completely dissolved. Add the flour and mix until you form a smooth dough. Cover the dough and leave it to rest in a warm dry place for 3 hours. At the end of every hour, press it down with a fork and leave it to rise again. Strip the rosemary needles from the stem, and chop them very finely with the sage leaves. Add them to the dough, along with the oregano and thyme and 5 twists of the pepper mill. Knead the dough until the herbs are evenly distributed. Heat the sunflower oil in a saucepan on a medium high heat. To check when the oil is hot enough for frying, drop in a small pinch of flour – if it sizzles and fries immediately, the oil is ready. Using two tablespoons, drop spoonfuls of dough into the hot oil and fry them for 3 minutes. Drain the dough balls on kitchen paper, sprinkle them with salt and serve immediately.

This fried dough has an intense, long-lasting taste. It is excellent as an appetiser served with salami and cheese, or use it to substitute bread to accompany aromatic roast meats.

Desserts

Sunshine's Panna Cotta

INGREDIENTS

20 fl oz/600 ml fresh
   double cream
3 tablespoons white sugar
tiny pinch of salt
½ lemon
½ oz/10 g gelatine or agar

GARNISH NO.1

3½ oz/100 g raspberries
2 oz/50 g blueberries
2½ oz/60 g flaked almonds

GARNISH NO.2

14 oz/400 g fresh strawberries
3 tablespoons organic brown
   sugar.
7 fl oz/200ml Marsala wine

Serves 5

Put the gelatine to soak in a bowl of cold water. Put the cream, pinch of salt and 3 tablespoons sugar into a small saucepan. Grate the rind of the half lemon into the cream and put the pan on a very low heat for 14 minutes, stirring gently all the time. The sugar needs to dissolve in the cream but do not allow the cream to boil because it will form a nasty skin on top. If you see vapour rising from the surface of the cream, this means it is reaching boiling point in which case take it off the heat and keep stirring it until it cools down a little. After 14 minutes, take the pan off the heat, lift the softened gelatine out of the soaking water and add it to the cream, stirring until it has dissolved. Divide the cream into 5 ramekins or glasses and leave it to cool to room temperature, at which point it needs to go in the fridge for at least 5 hours in order to set properly.

GARNISH NO.1

This garnish is very easy and very pretty. Put some raspberries and blueberries on top of the panna cotta, and scatter almond flakes over it. This is an explosion of sensations in the mouth – the intense forest fruits, the crunchiness of the almonds and the smooth creaminess of the panna cotta contrasting with the tart freshness of the lemon and sweetness of the sugar.

GARNISH NO.2

This garnish is also very simple. Cut the strawberries into small pieces and put them in a pan with the sugar. Caramelise lightly on a medium heat. After about 3 minutes pour over the Marsala wine, and cook for another 5 minutes, at which point the strawberries should be syrupy. Leave to cool a little and then put in the fridge for a few hours. When the panna cotta is ready, top it with the strawberries in Marsala wine and serve. You could also sprinkle some finely chopped hazelnuts on top.

Classic Tiramisù, My Style

INGREDIENTS

17½ oz/500 g mascarpone

6 large fresh organic eggs

60 Savoiardi or ladyfinger
   biscuits

11 tablespoons sugar

16 fl oz/500 ml coffee

5 fl oz/150 ml dry
   Marsala wine

organic cocoa powder

Serves 10

Make the coffee – half espresso and half filter coffee. When it has cooled, add a tablespoon of sugar and the Marsala wine, and stir until the sugar dissolves. Separate the egg whites and yolks in two glass bowls. Add 10 generous spoons of sugar to the yolks, and whisk until smooth. Add the mascarpone cheese and stir again until there are no visible lumps of mascarpone. Whisk the egg whites until they form stiff peaks and then fold them into the egg and mascarpone mix, always folding from low to high at a steady pace so as not to knock the air out of the egg whites. When everything is combined into a smooth cream, you are ready to assemble the tiramisu. You can make it in a baking dish, in individual ramekins, in glasses or whatever type of container you like. Dip a Savoiardi biscuit in the cold coffee for 3 seconds and then pull it out. Make a layer of coffee-dipped biscuits, cover it with half the mascarpone cream, then make a second layer of biscuits and finish with a layer of the remaining cream. Sprinkle with organic cocoa powder and optional plain chocolate chops to garnish. Refrigerate for at least 4 or 5 hours. Tiramisù is also very good the day after it is made, so it can be convenient to prepare it the day before you need it. In my experience, after two days it begins to deteriorate so don't keep it any longer than that.

ANOTHER VERSION – ORANGE TIRAMISÙ

This recipe is the same as the previous one, but uses blood orange juice instead of coffee for soaking the biscuits. You'll need 20 fl oz/600 ml of juice with the usual amount of Marsala wine and a tablespoon of sugar. Use freshly-squeezed juice or orange juice with no added sugar because otherwise your tiramisu will be too sweet and cloying. Serve garnished with a slice of orange. I wanted to include this version for those who don't like coffee, or as an alternative for children, in which case you should obviously also omit the Marsala wine. Try it!

Dark Chocolate Mousse with Forest Fruits, Cinnamon and Brown Sugar

INGREDIENTS

6½ oz/180 g plain chocolate

2½ oz/60 g butter

5 large organic eggs

3 tablespoons brown sugar

½ teaspoon cinnamon powder

(or grated orange rind or chilli
  powder)

Serves 6

Separate the egg yolks from the whites. Break the dark chocolate into pieces and cut the butter into chunks, and melt them together in a bain-marie or a heat-proof bowl over a pan of boiling water. Add the egg yolks one at a time, stirring vigorously. The mixture will thicken slightly, at which point take it off the heat and add the brown sugar and the powdered cinnamon (or spice of your choice), and mix well until it is smooth. Beat the egg whites until they are stiff and fold them into the chocolate cream. As you do this the mousse will become paler and paler, ending up a light brown. Divide the mousse among the serving ramekins or glasses or bowls or whatever you are using. Put them in the fridge for at least 5 hours. Serve the mousse garnished with raspberries and blueberries and chopped pistachios, or redcurrants, blueberries and flaked almonds, or as a third option try strawberries, blackberries and chopped hazelnuts. As usual, I have given you several ideas for different spices and toppings, but the basic recipe is always the same.

This mousse is very similar to the Kousmine-method mousse. Catherine Kousmine was a wonderful woman, a Russian doctor who moved to Switzerland to pursue her lifelong investigations into food and its effects on our health. In this recipe, I have suggested the classic cinnamon version and given you the orange and chilli options. Three different ingredients that give rise to three different recipes, and my heartfelt advice would be to try all three.

Tuscan Apple Cake

INGREDIENTS

5 apples (Golden Delicious variety or similar)

6½ oz/180 g sugar

3 large eggs

3 oz/80 g butter

5 oz/150 g 00 flour or fine-milled plain flour

3 oz/80 g raisins

2½ oz/60 g pine nuts or blanched almonds or walnuts

1 lemon

¾ oz sachet dried yeast (approx16 g)

4 fl oz/125 ml fresh milk

1 pinch of salt

1 teaspoon cinnamon powder

Serves 8

Preheat the oven to 200°C/400°F. Peel the apples, core them and slice them very thinly, and put the slices in a bowl of cold water so they don't go brown. Beat the eggs in a large glass bowl together with the sugar, melted butter and flour. When this is smoothly blended, add the raisins and pine nuts, or instead of the pine nuts you can use almonds or walnuts. Again, you have three options so you can make this cake three times to decide which one you prefer. When you use almonds or walnuts they should be roughly chopped, but the pine nuts are always used whole. Grate the lemon rind into the cake batter, then add a pinch of salt and a teaspoon of cinnamon powder and mix well. Dissolve the yeast in the milk and it will start to form a froth. ATTENTION! When you put the yeast into the milk, wait one minute before stirring it. The frothing effect will be less violent and better for our cake. Mix the milk and yeast into the cake batter and then stir in the apple slices. Pour the batter into a 11in/28cm circular baking pan, lined with baking paper. Put the cake in the preheated oven for 45 minutes. It is better not to use a fan-assisted oven. This cake does not need any further garnish or filling because the quantity of apples will make it perfectly moist as it is.

Cantuccini or Prato Biscuits
Served with Vin Santo

INGREDIENTS

12¾ oz/360 g 00 flour
  or fine-milled plain flour
12¾ oz/360 g sugar
3 medium eggs
½ teaspoon baking powder
1 pinch of salt
5 oz/150 g very finely
  chopped unpeeled almonds

Serves 8

Preheat the oven to 180°C/350°F. Mix the flour and sugar and pile it onto your work surface in a crater shape, or a volcano as I like to call it. Break the eggs into the centre of the volcano and add a pinch of salt and the baking powder. Using a fork, whisk the eggs until they are smoothly blended, and then start to incorporate the flour little by little from around the rim of the crater until it forms a dough that can be kneaded by hand. If necessary, add a little flour to stop the dough sticking to the work surface. Pour the finely chopped almonds on top of the dough and knead it until they are evenly distributed and the dough is smooth. Divide the dough into 6 pieces and roll each piece into a flattened sausage shape about 3 fingers wide and one finger high. Line a baking tray with baking paper and put the rolls of dough on it. Brush them lightly with egg yolk and bake for about 15 minutes at 180°C/350°F. Depending on your oven, they may need a little longer – 15 minutes is sufficient in a professional oven, but you may have to wait a little longer when using a domestic oven. The dough needs to be baked solid enough to be lifted off the tray without breaking. Turn the oven up to 190°C/375°F, and while it is heating put the rolls of dough on your work surface and cut them on the diagonal into ¾in/2cm wide slices. Spread the slices out on the tray again and put them back in the oven at 190°C/375°F for another 5 minutes. This double cooking method is why they are called 'biscuits' – from 'bis' which means twice and 'cuit' which means cooked.

In Tuscany, you will usually see Prato biscuits or cantuccini biscuits

made with whole almonds, but I prefer to use them finely chopped. The reason for this is that, unlike many chefs, I don't put grated lemon rind in my cantuccini. When we make homemade biscuits without butter, like these ones, the taste of the egg can be too strong, so to cover this sometimes unpleasant taste I chop the almonds finely so that they release more taste into the biscuits during cooking, and the final result is a delicious explosion of almond fragrance when you eat them.

Both in Italy and abroad these delicious biscuits are commonly known as 'cantucci' or 'cantuccini', but their real name is Prato biscuits, because that is the city in which they were born.

Prato is a city very close to Florence, famous for its pastries and high fashion textile industry. Returning to our biscuits, the traditional way to serve them is with "vin santo" dessert wine, but they are also wonderful with coffee, tea, milk or cappuccino.

CHOCOLATE CANTUCCINI OR PRATO BISCUITS
This recipe is the same as the previous one, except that we substitute 5½ oz/160 g of plain chocolate chips for the almonds. Simple, no?

Castagnaccio

INGREDIENTS

12½ oz/350 g chestnut flour

16 fl oz/500 ml cold water

1 tablespoon sugar

3 tablespoons extra-virgin
   olive oil

1 orange

3 sprigs of rosemary
   4in/10cm long

1½ oz/40 g pine nuts

1½ oz/40 g walnuts

Pinch of salt

Serves 5

Preheat the oven to 190°C/375°F. Sift the chestnut flour into a bowl, add the water and stir well. Grate the orange rind into the batter, then add 1 tablespoon of olive oil, a tablespoon of sugar and a pinch of salt, mix thoroughly and let the batter rest for about 2 hours. The chestnut flour could easily form lumps when you mix it with the water, in which case use a blender for just a few seconds to break them up. Line a 11in/28cm diameter circular baking pan with baking paper and grease it with a little extra virgin olive oil. Pour the batter into the pan, break the walnuts into pieces and sprinkle on top, along with the pine nuts and some rosemary needles. Drizzle with 3 tablespoons of extra virgin olive oil and bake for about 40 minutes. Castagnaccio should be served with fresh sheeps' milk ricotta cheese. Not everyone likes castagnaccio – it has a strong and unique taste, but when I teach my cooking courses I do prepare castagnaccio precisely so that my students can experience its uniqueness. The secret to a good castagnaccio is in the flour – use an excellent chestnut flour and the results are guaranteed. It is a Tuscan dessert but is eaten really in every mountainous region in Italy. I was born in Liguria, but I remember as a child we ate castagnaccio. This is an ancient recipe, and there are many stories and legends about its origins, but the first recorded castagnaccio recipe is usually attributed to a gentleman named Pilade who came from Lucca. I have given you the version of the recipe that I love, and I ask you to love it too, because it's worth it. I want this ancient and wonderful Tuscan dessert to live on. Make castagnaccio, and time will stand still.

Chestnut Heart Cake

INGREDIENTS

4 large organic eggs

1 small pot natural yoghurt
(4½ oz/125 g)

2 pots organic brown sugar

2 pots 00 flour or fine-milled
plain flour

2 pots stone-ground chestnut
flour

1 pot organic sunflower seed oil

½ pot milk or rice milk

1 sachet dried yeast
(¾ oz/16 g)

Serves 8

Preheat the oven to 180°C/350°F. **This recipe uses a 4 fl oz/125 ml yogurt pot to measure all the ingredients.** Break the eggs into a bowl, add the yogurt and then use the empty pot to measure the sugar, add it and mix thoroughly. Sieve the plain flour and chestnut flour into the batter and amalgamate them, making sure there are no lumps. Stir in the oil. Put the yeast into the milk and wait a minute before stirring, let it froth then pour the milk into the batter and mix until the batter is completely smooth and lump-free. Line a 10¼in/26cm diameter circular baking pan and line it with baking paper. Pour the cake batter in, and bake for 45 minutes. You can serve this cake with some melted chocolate and strawberries and raspberries to garnish, or with whipped cream and ricotta cheese.

This cake is like a childhood memory. When you make it, it will fill your kitchen with a fragrance that will make you daydream.

Sweet Focaccia or "Schiaccia" With Canaiola Grapes

INGREDIENTS

10 fl oz/300 ml warm water
1 pinch of salt
3 oz/80 g sugar
1 oz/9 g yeast
2 teaspoons extra-virgin olive oil
19 oz/550 g 0 grade flour or
   plain flour
7 oz/200 g Canaiola grapes

Serves 8

Preheat the oven to 200°C/400°F. Mix the warm water, pinch of salt, sugar, yeast and extra-virgin olive oil in a bowl. When the sugar and yeast have dissolved, sieve in the flour and mix until you have a soft and somewhat sticky dough. Cover and leave to rise for 3 hours in a warm, dry place. At the end of every hour, flatten the dough with a fork and leave it to rise again. Line a 15¾ in/40cm diameter circular baking pan with baking paper and grease it lightly. Put the soft dough in the centre of the pan. Flatten it with your hands, which you should also lightly grease with olive oil so the dough does not stick to them. Press it out until it covers the base of the pan. Wash and dry the grapes, then break them open one by one and squash them into the dough. Hence the name of this sweet focaccia-type bread – from the Italian verb 'schiacciare', to squash or crush, recalling both the squashing of the dough into the pan and the squashing of the grapes into the dough. If you can't find Canaiola grapes, use any small red juicy grape, preferably a variety that is used for winemaking. Sprinkle a little sugar over the dough – not too much, because we want to taste the natural sweetness of the grape sugar and not just the refined sugar on top – and bake for about 25 minutes.

Enjoy your schiaccia with some vin santo dessert wine or a glass of good Chianti wine. This rustic dessert was traditionally made in the period of the grape harvest. Serve it with a smile.

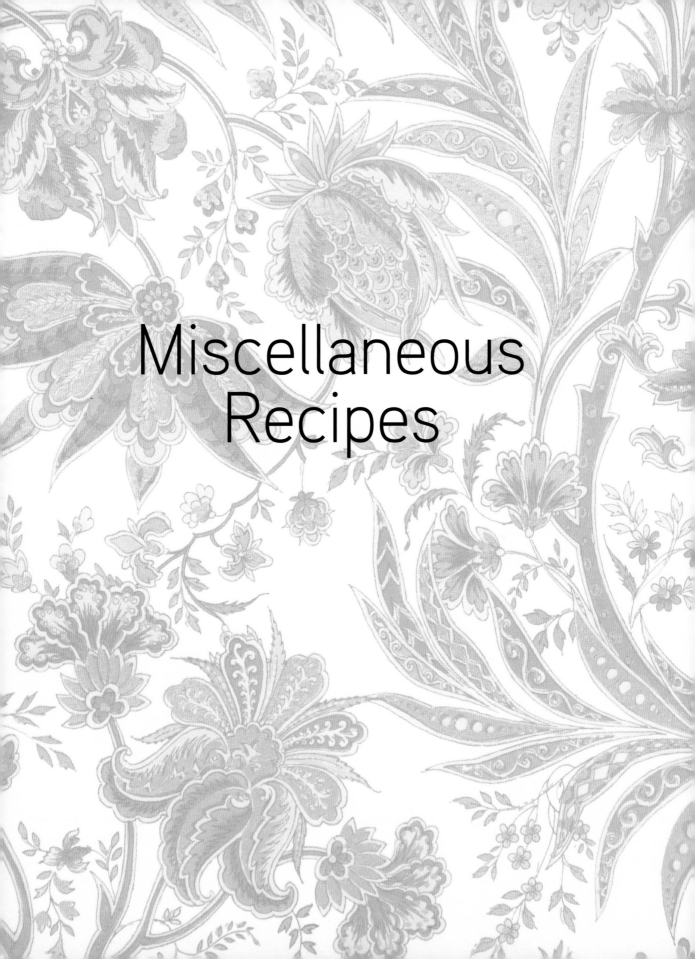

Miscellaneous Recipes

Gnocchi or "Gnudi", Casentino Style

INGREDIENTS

17½ oz/500 g spinach leaves

17½ oz/500 g chard leaves

14 oz/400 g fresh sheep's
milk ricotta cheese

2 medium eggs

3 oz/80 g grated Parmesan
cheese

2 oz/50 g breadcrumbs

white pepper

nutmeg, salt

Serves 5

Wilt the spinach and chard in boiling salted water. Drain, allow to cool, and squeeze out as much water as possible. Chop the leaves very finely and then mix in the sheep's milk ricotta cheese, Parmesan cheese, breadcrumbs, eggs, white pepper, nutmeg and salt. Amalgamate all these ingredients well until the mixture is smooth and lump-free. Roll it into 2in/5cm balls and flour them lightly with plain flour. Cook the gnocchi in abundant boiling salted water for about 5 minutes. Serve them piping hot – either in vegetable stock no.4 (page 71), or a sage butter dressing with a sprinkling of gated Parmesan cheese, or in a tomato and basil sauce.

You could also make a little béchamel sauce, arrange the gnocchi in a baking dish, pour over the béchamel, sprinkle with grated Parmesan cheese and then put the dish in the oven at 200°C/400°F for 10 minutes or until the cheese is melted and golden.

This is an important recipe from the Casentino area in the province of Arezzo, but it is also very popular around Lucca.

Potato Tortelli with Tuscan Beef Ragù, Mugello Style

INGREDIENTS FOR THE SAUCE

28 oz/700 g beef mince,

2½ oz/60 g celery

3 oz/80 g carrot

3 oz/80 g onion

2 medium cloves garlic

1 sprig fresh rosemary
3¼in/8cm long

3 medium sage leaves

5 oz/150 g organic tinned
peeled tomatoes

2 fl oz/50 ml white wine

2 fl oz/50 ml red wine

2 cloves

1 small piece cinnamon stick

1 bay leaf

9 tablespoons extra-virgin
olive oil

vegetable stock no.2 (page 70)

Serves 5

Chop the celery, carrot, onion, garlic, rosemary and sage very finely, and fry in extra-virgin olive oil for at least 10 minutes, with the cloves, cinnamon and bay leaf. Add the beef mince and fry on a medium heat until the meat browns and releases its liquid. Pour over the white wine and red wine, and cover everything with vegetable stock no.2. Why do I use two wines? Because the white wine gives a delicate taste while the red wine gives body and structure. Remember that a good ragù shouldn't be bright red – the tomato shouldn't dominate over the other ingredients. Every recipe of mine is a harmonious combination of ingredients that complement each other in the right proportions.

When the wine has evaporated (there is no more smell of alcohol), add the tinned tomatoes which you have crushed into pieces by hand. Cover and simmer the ragù for at least 3 hours, adding vegetable stock no.2 as necessary to prevent the ragù from becoming too dry. Add salt, white pepper and nutmeg to taste. Always simmer a ragù on a low heat – it has to cook very slowly, so meanwhile you can read a book, listen to music, paint, daydream – nourish your spirit while your nourishing ragù is cooking, calmly, with no rush. The ragù should be creamy, not watery when it is fully cooked. Have faith in its beauty.

FOR THE PASTA

4 large eggs

17½ oz/500 g 0 grade flour
   or plain flour

4 tablespoons warm water

3 teaspoons extra-virgin
   olive oil

2 pinches of salt

FOR THE FILLING

28 oz/700 g floury potatoes

2 large eggs

5 oz/150 g grated Parmesan
   cheese

3½ oz/100 g breadcrumbs

white pepper, nutmeg, salt

Make the pasta dough following the usual method, as explained in the previous chapter.

Cook the unpeeled potatoes in boiling salted water. When you can pierce a potato easily with a fork, they are cooked. Drain them and leave them to cool, then peel and mash them with a fork. Put the mashed potato in a large bowl, add the Parmesan cheese, bread crumbs, eggs, white pepper, nutmeg and salt and mix thoroughly until evenly blended. Taste the filling – some people like more or less nutmeg or pepper, but the important thing is balance, and no single ingredient should overpower the others.

Make the tortelli following the procedure given in the previous recipes, and cook them in abundant boiling salted water for about 8 minutes. Test to make sure they are cooked – when the pasta border of the tortelli is cooked to perfection, they are ready. Drain them and serve them piping hot with a drizzle of extra-virgin olive oil and the beef ragù on top. Sprinkle with Parmesan cheese to serve, but this is optional – I would advise you to try them both with and without cheese.

The Mugello is the mountainous part of the province of Florence, which borders on the province of Bologna. This recipe was born from the peasant cuisine of this rural area, just like the previous Lunigiana ravioli, but today we could say it is a royal dish in Florentine cuisine, and surprisingly good. One variation you could try is to add 7 oz/200 g of finely chopped pancetta to the filling, adding it to the fried vegetables and herbs at the start of the recipe. You can also serve these tortelli with the duck sauce from the chapter on Fresh Pasta, or dressed in butter and sage, or simply extra-virgin olive oil and thyme, or try them with a cherry tomato and basil sauce.

Tuscan Baked Maccheroni Pie

INGREDIENTS FOR THE PASTRY

9 oz/260 gr 0 grade flour or
  plain flour
3¾ oz/110 g butter
2 organic eggs
1 rounded tablespoon sugar
1 flat tablespoon salt

INGREDIENTS FOR THE FILLING

10½ oz/300 g top quality
  dried rigatoni or short tube-
  shaped pasta
24½ oz/700 g Tuscan meat
  ragù, see recipe on page 232
2 organic eggs
5¼ oz/150 g grated
  Parmesan cheese, black
  pepper, salt

Serves 8

Prepare the shortcrust pastry. Leave the butter out of the fridge until it is soft at room temperature. Crumble together the flour, butter, sugar and salt by hand, until the mixture resembles fine breadcrumbs. Pile it on your work surface and form it into a volcano shape. Break the eggs into the crater, whisk them with a fork, and then gradually incorporate the flour mixture and knead until you obtain a smooth dough. Cover it and leave to rest at room temperature for 1 hour.

Make the Tuscan ragù and allow to cool to room temperature. Cook the pasta in abundant boiling salted water. When it is cooked al dente, drain it and set aside to cool. Put the pastry on a sheet of baking paper, and roll it out to a thickness of about ½ cm. Place it in a 25cm diameter circular baking pan or pie dish. Prick the pastry all over with a fork.

Now we can start to assemble the finished dish. Put the cooled pasta in a large bowl, mix in the ragù sauce, 2 beaten eggs, grated Parmesan cheese, black pepper and a pinch of salt. If you like cinnamon, you can add a little to taste. Mix everything together well and then pour it into the pie dish. Turn the edges of the pastry slightly over the filling and sprinkle some more grated Parmesan cheese all over the pie.

Bake at 170°C for about 30 minutes. Let the pie cool slowly before slicing it, as the pastry will break if it's sliced while too hot. You can make this dish the day before you need it, then warm it up a

little before serving. It's delicious and visually very attractive. Some versions of this recipe include a béchamel sauce to bind the pasta together, but I find that makes it too rich and heavy. If the filling is mixed really well so all the pasta is coated in ragù sauce and egg, then the béchamel sauce is not necessary.

This recipe originates around the city of Ferrara in Emilia Romagna, but is also very popular in Tuscany. It can also be done with a pigeon ragù, or in a vegetarian version with a vegetable ragù and béchamel sauce, or try using a meat ragù without any tomato. An important recipe, which opens the door to many variations whilst respecting the basic procedure.

Braised Pork Ribs or "Rosticciana" with Olives

INGREDIENTS

45 oz/1.3 kg pork ribs

3 oz/80 g onion

2 large cloves garlic

3 sprigs rosemary, about
   6in/15cm long

15 medium sage leaves

3 bay leaves

7 tablespoons extra-virgin
   olive oil

7 fl oz/200 ml dry white wine

vegetable stock no.5 (page 72)

40 Tuscan olives in brine (or
   Kalamata olives)

14 oz/400 g organic tinned
   peeled tomatoes

white pepper, nutmeg, salt

Serves 5

Cut the ribs into 2in/5cm pieces. Chop the onion, garlic, rosemary and sage leaves very finely, and fry in extra-virgin olive oil for about 7 minutes, along with the bay leaves. Lightly flour the ribs and add them to the pan, browning them on all sides. Pour over the white wine and then enough vegetable stock no. 5 to cover the meat. When the wine has evaporated and there is no more smell of alcohol coming from the pan, add the olives. Crush the tomatoes by hand into small pieces and add them too. Stir, cover, and simmer for about 1 hour. Check for salt, and add some if needed – be careful, as the olives will have released their salt into the sauce so you probably don't need to add much more. Stir in a sprinkling of nutmeg and white pepper. When the meat is practically falling off the bone, it is ready.

In the Tuscan countryside pork ribs or 'rosticciana' are often simply grilled or barbecued, but there are several variations on this braised version which I will give you in future books.

Family Recipes

Mussels "Alla Marinara" by Uncle Salvatore, also known as "George"

INGREDIENTS

70 oz/2 kg medium sized very fresh mussels

4 medium cloves garlic

3 tablespoons finely chopped parsley

3 small chilli peppers

6 tablespoons extra-virgin olive oil

3¼ fl oz/100 ml Vermentino dry white wine

20 oz/600 g of cherry tomatoes

white pepper

salt

Serves 5

Rinse and clean the mussels, removing any beards. Quarter the cherry tomatoes. Chop the garlic and chilli peppers very finely, and mix with the chopped parsley. Put the olive oil in a big pan and heat it on a medium heat for about 2 minutes. Add the mussels, cover the pan and as soon as the mussels start to open, add the chopped garlic, chilli and parsley. Stir and cook for another 2 minutes. Pour over the wine and evaporate it for 5 minutes, then add the cherry tomatoes, white pepper and a little salt. Cook for another 8 minutes and your mussels are ready. Serve hot with slices of toasted bread rubbed with garlic. Thanks Uncle Salvatore, as usual I followed my head and heart and modified your recipe a little, but its soul is intact.

Grandma Emy's Stuffed Zucchinis

INGREDIENTS

10 medium zucchinis (courgette)

14 oz/400 g floury potatoes

2 medium organic eggs

1 tablespoon finely chopped parsley

2½ oz/60 g grated Parmesan cheese

3 tablespoons breadcrumbs

1 clove garlic

3 tablespoons extra-virgin olive oil

2½ oz/60 g dried porcini mushrooms

white pepper, salt

Serves 5

Grandma Emy makes these stuffed zucchinis every time she visits us in Tuscany.

Preheat the oven to 180°C/350°F. Boil the potatoes in their skins, drain and leave to cool a little, then peel and mash them. Soak the mushrooms in warm water for about 20 minutes, then rinse them thoroughly to remove any earth or impurities, squeeze them out well and chop them roughly. Cut the zucchinis in half lengthwise and boil them in salted water for about 3 minutes, then lay them flat side down on a tea-towel to dry. Hollow out the zucchinis using a knife or teaspoon, making them into kind of boat shapes ready to be filled. Fry the whole garlic clove in a pan with the extra virgin olive oil. Add the mushrooms, and fry for about 2 minutes then remove the garlic, add the mashed potatoes and mix well. Add the eggs, breadcrumbs, Parmesan cheese, chopped parsley, white pepper and salt. Mix thoroughly to amalgamate all the ingredients evenly.

Fill the zucchini boats with this mixture. Line a baking pan with baking paper, grease it lightly with olive oil and arrange the zucchinis in rows. Sprinkle a little more grated Parmesan cheese on top and bake until the zucchinis are golden and the cheese is melted.

Thank you Emy for this recipe you have given us, but I'm going to need more recipes very soon for the next book. After all our ups and downs, dear mother, who would have thought we'd be taking your simple but excellent cooking around the world. One of life's wonderful surprises.

Gemma's Scarpaccia

INGREDIENTS

7 oz/200 g pale zucchinis
   (courgettes)

1 clove garlic

5 tablespoons extra-virgin
   olive oil

15 basil leaves

2 sprigs of nepitella

white pepper, nutmeg

1 tablespoon flour

2 fl oz/50 ml water

2 oz/50 g grated Parmesan
   cheese

Serves 2

Preheat the oven to 200°C/400°F. Roughly chop the basil leaves. Wash and dry the zucchinis, and slice them as thinly as possible – the discs of zucchini should be almost transparent. Fry them in a pan with extra-virgin olive oil over a medium high heat for a few minutes, then add the basil, nepitella leaves, salt, pepper and nutmeg to taste. Cook for 10 minutes, then add the water and Parmesan cheese, and sprinkle over the flour. Stir well and put the mixture into a 10in/25cm diameter circular baking pan lined with baking paper, and put it in the preheated oven for about 7 minutes. When the zucchinis are golden brown, the scarpaccia is ready. This is Gemma's savoury scarpaccia, Camaiore style, delicate but tasty. When I visit Gemma we sit by the fireplace and tell old stories, eating scarpaccia accompanied by pecorino cheese, olives and of course some good wine. In Viareggio in the province of Lucca, scarpaccia is made with sugar and it is a very particular type of sweet dessert made with vegetables, but this savoury version is closer to the recipe from Camaiore, a town in the Versilia area of Lucca province. I love it. You can use it as a starter, or cut it into squares for an appetiser or finger food. Simply fantastic.

Aunt Maria's Lamb Cutlets: Marinated, Breaded And Fried

This recipe does not serve a specific number of people. I will explain why.

INGREDIENTS

20 lamb cutlets

3 large organic eggs

2 medium cloves garlic

3 sprigs of rosemary
about 6in/15cm long

12 large sage leaves

black pepper, salt

20 oz/600 g
breadcrumbs

1¾ pint/1 litre organic
sunflower seed oil

Whisk the eggs in a large bowl. Use a meat hammer or base of a bottle to flatten the cutlets slightly. Put them in the bowl with the eggs and use your hands to turn the cutlets until they are all coated in egg. Strip the rosemary needles from the stem and chop them very finely along with the garlic and the sage leaves. Add to the lamb, along with salt and pepper and mix everything again with your hands. Cover and leave to rest in the fridge for at least 5 hours. Take the meat out of the fridge and mix it one more time. Meanwhile heat the olive oil in a frying pan – to test if it is at the correct temperature for frying, drop a small pinch of breadcrumbs into the oil. If they sizzle and fry immediately, the oil is hot enough. Put all the breadcrumbs on a large plate and press both sides of each cutlet into them. Fry the cutlets until they are golden brown, as in the photo. The cooking time depends very much on the size and thickness of the cutlets, but probably around 5 minutes. Drain the cutlets on kitchen paper to absorb any excess oil, and serve hot, sprinkled with salt and accompanied by a green salad. These crispy lamb cutlets are simply amazingly delicious. I haven't been able to specify how many people this recipe would serve, because it very much depends on the people! When I was younger, I could eat all 20 cutlets and possibly more. If you like lamb, you won't be able to stop eating these. A restaurant portion would be 3 cutlets, as in the photo. I always teach this recipe in my cooking courses, and it is always eaten with great enthusiasm.

Thanks to Aunt Maria for the hundreds and hundreds of lamb cutlets she fried over so many Christmases and Easters and feast days, in her small but magical kitchen. My thanks for your passion and devotion!

Spaghetti by Grandma Cira, also known as "Tweetypie"

INGREDIENTS

17½ oz/500 g top quality
    spaghetti
35 oz/1 kg mussels
35 oz/1 kg clams
10 shrimps (prawns)
2 medium cloves garlic
2 small dried chilli peppers
1 tablespoon chopped parsley
7 tablespoons extra-virgin
    olive oil
7 fl oz/200 ml dry white wine
vegetable stock no.1 (page 70)
salt

Serves 5

Put the clams in a bowl of water with a pinch of salt for an hour. Rinse the mussels and remove any beards. Remove the heads from 5 of the shrimps and simmer them in the vegetable stock no.1. Chop the garlic and chilli peppers very finely, and fry in a large pan in extra-virgin olive oil for about 1 minute. Add the mussels, the clams and the shrimps (5 with heads, 5 without). Cover the pan, and as soon as the mussels and clams start to open, pour over the white wine. Add a pinch of salt and the chopped parsley. Cook for about 10 minutes then take off the heat. Lift out the 5 headless shrimps, 10 mussels and 15 clams. Peel the shrimps and remove the mussels and clams from their shells. Chop shrimps, clams and mussels finely with a knife, to obtain a very tasty seafood mixture or 'battuto'.

Cook the spaghetti in abundant boiling lightly salted water. Drain it 2 minutes before the end of cooking time, and toss it in the pan with the seafood sauce and a little of the shrimp-enriched vegetable stock. When the spaghetti is perfectly cooked, stir in the chopped mixture of mussels, clams and shrimps.

Grandma Cira, also known as Tweetypie, just like the cartoon canary, makes these delicious spaghetti which are quite unique because of the finely chopped seafood 'battuto' technique. It's an excellent recipe to use with fresh egg tagliolini pasta, well worth trying.

Grandpa Nino's Tagliolini with Meat and Mushroom Ragù

INGREDIENTS FOR THE PASTA

5 large eggs

17½ oz/500 g durum wheat
   flour

2 pinches of salt

4 tablespoons warm water

INGREDIENTS FOR THE SAUCE

14 oz/400 g mince

3½ oz/100 g sausage

2 oz/50 g onion

2 oz/50 g carrot

2 oz/50 g celery

3 oz/80 g pine nuts

6 tablespoons extra-virgin
   olive oil

3 oz/80 g dried porcini
   mushrooms

10½ oz/300 g organic
   tinned peeled tomatoes

2 bay leaves, 3 large sage
   leaves

1 sprig rosemary about
   6in/15cm long

black pepper, nutmeg, salt

Serves 5

Grandpa Nino never weighs anything when he cooks, and his portions are always ample! I'll give you the quantities to help you. Put the flour on your work surface and make it into a volcano, then break the eggs into it and add the salt and water. Whisk the eggs with a fork, and when they are smoothly blended gradually incorporate the flour from around the edge of the crater until you have a dough that is solid enough to be kneaded until it is smooth and elastic. Grandpa Nino usually rolls out the dough with a pasta machine and then cuts it into tagliolini. He sprinkles the tagliolini with durum wheat flour to stop them from sticking to each other, spreads them out on his work surface and covers them with a clean tea-towel until the sauce is ready.

PROCEDURE FOR THE SAUCE

If possible, make this sauce in an earthenware stove-top pot that can be used on direct heat. Otherwise your usual saucepan will do. Soak the mushrooms in warm water for at least 20 minutes then rinse them thoroughly to remove any remaining earth and impurities, squeeze them out well and chop them roughly with a knife. Heat the extra-virgin olive oil and fry the pine nuts until they turn golden brown. Chop the onion, carrot and celery very finely and add to the pan. Fry for about 3 minutes then add the mince and squeeze the sausage meat out of its casing into the pan. Break the mince and sausage meat up with a wooden spoon as they cook. Strip the rosemary needles from the stem and chop them very finely along with the sage leaves. When the meat has browned, add the herbs, the tomatoes crushed into pieces, and salt and pepper to taste. Simmer for about 20 minutes then add the bay leaves and the mushrooms. Simmer for another hour.

This recipe is the jewel in grandpa Nino's culinary crown. The sauce is also very good with polenta or with Lunigiana ravioli or vegetable ravioli. See the chapter Fresh Stuffed Pasta.

Grandma Nunzia's Neapolitan Pastiera

INGREDIENTS FOR THE PASTRY

17½ oz/500 g plain flour

5 oz/150 g sugar

2 medium eggs

9 oz/250 g butter

1 pinch of salt

INGREDIENTS FOR THE FILLING

16 oz/450 g cooked wheat

16 fl oz/500 ml milk

knob of butter

½ lemon

17½ oz/500 g fresh cow
   ricotta cheese

14 oz/400 g sugar

6 egg yolks, 6 egg whites

½ teaspoon ground cinnamon

½ teaspoon vanilla essence

1 teaspoon orange blossom
   water

Serves 8

Mix the flour and sugar in a large bowl, chop the butter into small pieces and add it to the bowl. Work the butter into the flour and sugar mix using your hands until the texture is like breadcrumbs. Make a volcano with it on your work surface – in the case of this recipe from Naples, we could call it Vesuvius – and break the 2 eggs into the crater. Add a pinch of salt and whisk the eggs until they are well blended, then gradually incorporate the flour mixture from around the edges of the crater until the dough is solid enough to knead with the hands. When it is smooth, wrap the ball of dough in cling-film and leave it to rest in the fridge for at least an hour. Your Neapolitan short crust pastry is ready.

PROCEDURE FOR THE FILLING

Preheat the oven to 140°C/285°F. Rinse the cooked wheat and drain it well. Put it in a pan with the milk, butter and a piece of lemon rind. Warm it on a low heat for about 20 minutes, stirring occasionally, until it becomes creamy. Remove the lemon rind then blend the wheat for a few seconds using a handheld blender. Put the ricotta cheese in a large glass or steel bowl with the sugar and beat vigorously with a fork or a whisk until it is smooth and creamy. Continue to whisk, adding the egg yolks one at a time, then add the cinnamon, vanilla essence and orange flower water and finally the creamy wheat, mixing all the time. In a separate bowl, beat the egg whites until stiff, then fold into the wheat mixture, always folding from low to high. Roll out the short crust pastry on a sheet of baking paper to about 4mm thickness, then put it into a circular cake pan, 12in/30cm diameter with sides 2in/5cm high. Pour in the filling and make a lattice of ½in/1cm wide pastry strips on top. Bake for about 1 hour, until the pastry is golden brown.

Grandma Nunzia prepares this Neapolitan pastiera on Holy Thursday, 3 days before Easter. The secret of the pastiera is that it needs to be cooked some days in advance, to allow the pastry to soften and the fragrances to mix properly, giving it that unique taste. It is then eaten on Easter Sunday. This is a classic Neapolitan tradition, every family in Naples eats pastiera at Easter. Grandma Nunzia also says it is traditional to put the pastiera on the table along with the appetisers before starting lunch. This is considered a good wish or a blessing for the family. It's a very special cake that has important spiritual significance in Naples.

Index

ACKNOWLEDGEMENTS

Daniela Auriuso digital photographer
Zara Nelson translator
Silvio Massolo, Villa la Selva
Tenuta Ricrio, Mammarò Lucca.

For my son Ettore, Silvana (love), Nino, Emy, Alfonso, Titti, Nunzia, Loredana, Caio, Fabiola, Leo, Dario, Frank Zappa, Puccini, Escargot, Gemma, Maria, Radiodervish, Salvatore, Orchestra di Piazza Vittorio, Fabrizio de Andrè.

CREDITS

Chopping very very finely
by Sunshine Manitto

Created, dreamed by Sunshine Manitto
Web site: www.sunshinechefintuscany.com

Photography copyright © Daniela Auriuso 2013
Web site: www.danielaauriuso.com

Zara Nelson, translator, editor and dancer
E-mail: zara.nelson@gmail.com

Editorial consultancy and coordination
Silvio Massolo
Web site: www.silviomassolo.com

SPECIAL THANKS

Tenuta Ricrio
Web site: www.tenutaricrio.it

Agriturismo La Selva
Web site: www.laselva.net

Mammarò Lucca
Web site: www.mammaro.com
Piazza Anfiteatro 4, Lucca

First published in 2015 by New Holland Publishers Pty Ltd
London • Sydney • Auckland

The Chandlery Unit 009 50 Westminster Bridge Road London SE1 7QY United Kingdom
1/66 Gibbes Street Chatswood NSW 2067 Australia
5/39 Woodside Ave Northcote Auckland 0627 New Zealand

www.newhollandpublishers.com

A record of this book is held at the British Library and the National Library of Australia.

ISBN 9781742576220

Managing Director: Fiona Schultz
Publisher: Alan Whiticker
Project Editor: Holly Willsher
Designer: Lorena Susak
Production Director: Olga Dementiev
Printer: Toppan Leefung Printing Ltd

10 9 8 7 6 5 4 3 2 1

Keep up with New Holland Publishers on Facebook
www.facebook.com/NewHollandPublishers

www.sunshinechefintuscany.com

UK £16.99
US $19.99